Table o

Amalfi Coast Travel Guide

The Ultimate Travel Guide For Planning Your Trip To Amalfi Coast From Where to stay, Things To Do, What To Pack, Food To Try Out etc

Enzo Luca

Brief History

The Amalfi Coast is a gorgeous stretch of coastline in southern Italy, located in the province of Salerno in the Campania region. It has a long history dating back to the Roman Empire and has been a popular tourist destination for centuries due to its spectacular natural beauty, beautiful seaside towns, and rich cultural legacy.

In Roman times, the area was famed for its production of paper, a valuable item in those days. In the 9th century, the coastal cities created a maritime republic known as the Duchy of Amalfi, which became a prominent trading power in the Mediterranean, particularly in the spice trade. During this time, the town of Amalfi was a hub of culture and commerce and had strong contact with the Arab world, as evidenced by its Arab-style architecture.

In the 11th and 12th centuries, the Amalfi Coast was devastated by Saracen pirates, leading to a collapse in its strength and economy. In the 16th century, the territory was dominated by Spain, followed by the Bourbons in the 18th century.

In the 20th century, the Amalfi Coast became a popular tourist destination, bringing visitors from around the world to its charming villages, rocky cliffs, and crystal-clear waters. Today, it remains one of Italy's most famous tourist attractions, with millions of visitors each year coming to appreciate its natural beauty, rich cultural legacy, and lovely seaside towns.

In 1997, the Amalfi Coast is designated a UNESCO World Heritage site, recognizing its unique cultural and natural splendor. The complex encompasses the towns of Amalfi, Positano, and Ravello, as well as the surrounding islands of Li Galli and the historic Roman harbor of Villa Jovis.

In addition to its natural beauty and rich cultural past, the Amalfi Coast is also famous for its cuisine, which is highly inspired by the sea and the region's bountiful agricultural productivity. Visitors can enjoy fresh seafood dishes, hand-made pasta, and locally-produced fruits and vegetables, as well as the famed limoncello liquor, derived from the lemons growing in the region.

Tourism is a key economy on the Amalfi Coast, with millions of people each year coming to discover its quaint towns, relax on its clean beaches, and walk its gorgeous trails. In recent years, there has been a growing trend of sustainable tourism, with many local businesses and groups seeking to conserve the area's natural beauty and cultural legacy while still delivering a positive experience for visitors.

The Amalfi Coast is also a popular setting for film and television shooting, with several Hollywood movies produced in the area, including the iconic James Bond film, "Spectre." The area's magnificent vistas and quaint coastal villages have also been the backdrop for countless fashion shots and ads.

The Amalfi Coast is a unique and fascinating region, with a rich history, spectacular natural beauty, and a thriving cultural legacy. It is one of Italy's most famous tourist sites and is a must-visit location for anybody interested in history, and culture, or simply seeking a quiet and revitalizing retreat.

Activities To Do Throughout The Year

The Amalfi Coast provides a selection of activities throughout the year. These are some of the most popular activities for tourists in Amalfi Coast:

January

Winter hiking: The mild winter temperatures make it a fantastic season for hiking and exploring the gorgeous coastal routes of the Amalfi Coast.

February

Carnivals: Some of the towns along the coast, such as Scala and Ravello, conduct spectacular carnivals during the month of February.

March

Easter Celebrations: Easter is an important festival in Italy and many communities along the coast host unique celebrations and religious events.

April - June

Beaches: As the weather starts to warm up, many tourists travel to the magnificent beaches along the coast, such as Praiano and Positano.

Boat tours: Boat trips around the coast are a popular pastime and give beautiful views of the cliff-lined shoreline.

July - August

Festivals: The Amalfi Coast is noted for its colorful festivals and events during the summer months, such as the Festa della Madonna della Libera in Atrani and the Festa dei Ferragosto in Praiano.

Swimming and water activities: The mild summer months are great for swimming and enjoying numerous water sports, such as kayaking and snorkeling.

September - October

Harvest Festival: The villages of the Amalfi Coast celebrate harvest festivals in September and October, including local food and wine.

Picturesque drives: The scenic drive along the Amalfi Coast is particularly attractive during the fall, with the changing leaves and cool weather.

November - December

Christmas celebrations: Many towns along the coast offer particular Christmas markets and activities, such as the Christmas lights in Positano and the Nativity scenes in Ravello.

Winter walks: The mild winter weather makes it a fantastic time for touring the picturesque cities and villages along the coast, such as Amalfi and Atrani.

Top Attractions City on Amalfi Coast

The Amalfi Coast is a renowned tourist destination in Italy noted for its charming villages, stunning coastline, and wonderful cuisine. Here are some of the popular tourist sites and food that the Amalfi Coast has to offer:

Positano

Positano is a lovely village famed for its spectacular cliff-side villas, narrow winding alleyways, and beautiful beaches. It's a popular tourist site, attracting tourists from all over the world with its lovely ambiance, colorful architecture, and stunning views.

One of the most striking features is its steep cliff-side buildings, which are painted in beautiful pastel colors, making the town look like a painting. Visitors can walk around the streets and take in the splendor of the town, stopping at various stores and eateries along the way. The main beach in Positano is named Spiaggia Grande and is a popular site for sunbathing, swimming, and water sports.

Another must-see is the Chiesa di Santa Maria Assunta, a church that goes back to the 13th century. The church is notable for its imposing dome and its exquisite majolica tiles, which depict the Transfiguration of Jesus. Visitors can also take a walk up to the church's terrace for panoramic views of the town.

For those who prefer shopping, Positano is a terrific location, with a choice of artisan shops that sell handmade ceramics, jewelry, apparel, and other items. Visitors can also try the local cuisine, featuring meals like seafood risotto, linguine alle vongole, and lemon sorbet, all produced with fresh ingredients from the adjacent shore and hills.

Positano is also a fantastic starting place for exploring other sites along the Amalfi Coast, including the neighboring towns of Amalfi, Ravello, and Sorrento. Visitors can take a ferry or a bus along the coast to explore these settlements, or they can hike along the gorgeous coastal paths for a unique perspective of the area.

Positano is a very unique and charming place, allowing tourists an opportunity to see the splendor of the Amalfi Coast in a relaxing, romantic atmosphere. Whether you're looking for a beach holiday, a romantic break, or a cultural adventure, Positano has something to offer everyone.

Best locations of lodging to stay in Positano

Positano Offers a variety of hotel alternatives to suit different budgets and preferences. Some of the nicest places to stay in Positano include:

Hotel Le Sirenuse: A magnificent hotel with stunning views of the Mediterranean, offering elegant rooms and suites, a restaurant, a bar, and a spa.

Hotel Il San Pietro di Positano: A 5-star hotel with breathtaking views, a private beach, and a rooftop infinity pool.

Villa TreVille: A boutique hotel built in a gorgeous cliffside location, offering elegant rooms and suites, a restaurant, and a beautiful garden with a pool.

Palazzo Murat: A historic hotel housed in a restored 18th-century palace, with spacious rooms and suites, a restaurant, and a swimming pool.

Casa Albertina: A wonderful bed & breakfast with spacious rooms, a magnificent terrace, and a garden with a pool.

These are some of the main hotel options in Positano, although there are many more to pick from, depending on your budget and interests.

Ravello

Ravello is a lovely hilltop hamlet noted for its amazing views of the Tyrrhenian Sea and stunning scenery. It is situated at an altitude of more than 300 meters above sea level, affording magnificent panoramas of the surrounding area. Ravello is famed for its rich cultural legacy and has been a popular tourist destination for many years.

One of the most prominent landmarks in Ravello is the Villa Rufolo, a 13th-century villa that was formerly home to one of the most powerful families in the area. Today, it functions as a cultural center and holds a variety of performances and exhibitions throughout the year. Another notable site is the Villa Cimbrone, a large villa that was erected in the 11th century and is now a hotel.

The villa is famous for its spectacular gardens, which offer stunning views of the coast and are considered to be one of the most beautiful in the world.

Ravello is also home to several churches, including the 11th-century Church of San Giovanni del Toro, which is one of the oldest in the area, and the Cathedral of Ravello, which was erected in the 12th century, and is considered to be one of the most beautiful cathedrals in the Amalfi Coast region. Visitors can also explore the Ravello Art Museum, which showcases a collection of local art and antiquities, and the Ravello Historic Center, which is filled with small cobblestone streets, ancient buildings, and breathtaking views of the surrounding countryside.

The town is surrounded by thick greenery and boasts several lovely parks and gardens, notably the Gardens of the Villa Rufolo, which include exotic flora and stunning views of the sea. Visitors can also take a walk through the Giardini di Augusto, a terraced garden that is considered one of the most beautiful in the area.

Ravello is also recognized for its superb local cuisine, which includes a range of fresh fish, pasta dishes, and sweet desserts. Visitors can enjoy traditional delicacies such as pasta with lemon and seafood, or sample the local limoncello, a sweet lemon liqueur that is derived from the famed lemons of the Amalfi Coast.

Despite its tiny size, Ravello is a center of cultural activity and is home to various cultural events throughout the year. The Ravello Festival is one of the most popular events that is held yearly in the summer months. The festival comprises a range of classical music concerts, dance performances, and cultural displays, and attracts tourists from all over the world.

Ravello is a picturesque town that is rich in history and culture and is regarded as one of the most stunning places on the Amalfi Coast. Its beautiful landscapes, rich past, and active cultural scene make it a must-visit destination for anybody visiting to Italy. Whether you are seeking beautiful views, wonderful food, or a rich cultural experience, Ravello has something for everyone.

Best places of lodging to stay in Ravello

There are several fantastic places to stay in Ravello, ranging from luxury hotels to more economical ones. Some of the nicest places to stay include:

Villa Maria - a beautiful and elegant hotel with stunning views of the sea and the surrounding countryside.

Palazzo Avino - a 5-star hotel with an outdoor pool and spectacular views of the coastline.

Hotel Caruso Is a magnificent 11th-century palace that has been turned into a beautiful hotel with stunning views and great service.

La Rondinaia Is a trendy and stylish property that offers beautiful views of the Amalfi Coast and the town of Ravello.

Villa Cimbrone Is a historic hotel with a calm position with spectacular views of the sea and the town of Ravello.

Regardless of your budget or tastes, Ravello offers a wide choice of lodging alternatives that are sure to suit your needs and exceed your expectations.

Sorrento

Sorrento is a city located on the southern shore of Italy's Bay of Naples, in the Campania region. It is a popular tourist attraction noted for its stunning views, attractive streets, and rich history.

One of the city's most notable monuments is the Piazza Tasso, which serves as the central square and is flanked by cafes, restaurants, and boutiques. From here, visitors may take in panoramic views of the Bay of Naples, Mount Vesuvius, and the island of Capri. The Corso Italia is Sorrento's principal shopping route, offering everything from trinkets to high-end designer retailers.

Sorrento is also recognized for its historic buildings, including the 13th-century Cathedral of Sorrento, which contains Gothic and Renaissance-style architecture, and the Chapel of San Francesco, which is noted for its magnificent murals.

One of the city's greatest draws is its gorgeous coastline cliffs and beaches, which offer a tranquil getaway from the crowded city core. The Marina Piccola is a popular site for swimming and sunbathing, while the rocky shoreline provides a stunning backdrop for a sunset promenade. The neighboring seaside towns of Positano and Amalfi are other popular day trip destinations and may be reached by ferry from Sorrento's marina.

It is also famed for its lemon orchards, which produce the prized Sorrento lemons used in local cuisine, and Limoncello, a popular Italian liquor. Visitors can take a tour of one of the local lemon groves to learn about the production process and enjoy the fresh fruit.

Sorrento is a hub for trips to neighboring locations, including the ancient city of Pompeii, the magnificent island of Capri, and the stunning Amalfi Coast itself.

Capri, located off the coast of Sorrento, is famed for its gorgeous scenery, turquoise waters, and stylish boutiques. The island may be reached by ferry or hydrofoil and provides a range of activities, including hiking, boat cruises, and sunbathing on its gorgeous beaches.

Sorrento's cuisine is an essential element of its cultural legacy, with local delicacies including fresh seafood dishes, Neapolitan-style pizza, and homemade pasta. Visitors can enjoy the local food at one of Sorrento's many restaurants, which range from traditional trattorias to luxury dining venues.

Sorrento is a lovely city that provides a unique blend of history, natural beauty, and local culture. Whether you're interested in discovering ancient ruins, soaking up the sun on a magnificent beach, or indulging in local food, Sorrento is the perfect spot for a memorable Italian holiday.

Best Places of Accommodation to stay in Sorrento

There are various possibilities for housing in Sorrento, ranging from budget-friendly hotels to opulent resorts. Some of the greatest places to stay in Sorrento include:

Grand Hotel Excelsior Vittoria: A historic 5-star hotel with a superb location on the cliff overlooking the Bay of Naples, offering stunning views and exquisite accommodations.

Hotel Luna Convento: A restored 16th-century offers exquisite rooms and a calm ambiance.

Villa Fiorentino: A magnificent villa with a stunning sea-view terrace, offering self-catering apartments and high-end amenities.

Hotel Antiche Mura: A lovely hotel set in a restored 19th-century building, located just steps from Sorrento's main center, and offers rooms with antique furnishings.

Home Degli Dei: A secluded villa surrounded by olive groves and lemon trees, offering spacious suites with private terraces and panoramic views.

Regardless matter where you choose to stay in Sorrento, you are sure to appreciate the magnificent surroundings, great cuisine, and rich cultural legacy of this picturesque Italian town.

Pompeii

Pompeii was a prosperous Roman metropolis located in what is now the modern-day region of Campania. The city was buried under meters of ash and pumice following the eruption of Mount Vesuvius in 79 AD, preserving the city's architecture, frescoes, mosaics, and other relics for centuries. As a result, Pompeii is one of the most famous archaeological sites in the world, attracting millions of visitors each year.

Pompeii was originally founded in the 7th or 6th century BC by the Oscans, and it became a Roman town around 80 BC. The city was famed for its luxury residences, public buildings, bathhouses, theaters, and amphitheaters, as well as its rich history, which is evidenced in the various inscriptions and monuments that have been found in the city.

The eruption of Mount Vesuvius in 79 AD was one of the most disastrous natural disasters in Roman history. The eruption lasted for two days, and the city of Pompeii was buried under a layer of ash and pumice that reached up to 20 meters in some areas. Despite the devastation, the ash and pumice that coated the city served to preserve the city's structures, frescoes, mosaics, and other artifacts, allowing us to see what life was like in ancient Rome.

Visitors to Pompeii can visit the city's well-preserved ruins, including the forum, the market, the bathhouses, the theaters, and the amphitheaters, as well as the numerous magnificent houses that have been excavated. Some of the more notable houses include the House of the Faun, the House of the Vettii, and the Villa of the Mysteries. The city's public buildings, including the temples, the basilicas, and the forum, are also of great interest to visitors since they provide an insight into the religious, political, and commercial life of ancient Rome.

Visitors can also visit many of the city's treasures, including frescoes, mosaics, and sculptures, in the neighboring Naples National Archaeological Museum. The museum is one of the biggest collections of Roman antiques in the world and is home to many of the most important and well-preserved pieces from Pompeii and other Roman cities.

Visitors to Pompeii can also explore the adjacent Mount Vesuvius, which is still an active volcano. A trip up the mountain affords beautiful views of the Bay of Naples and the surrounding countryside, as well as an opportunity to learn about the volcano's history.

Pompeii is a must-visit location for anybody interested in ancient Roman history and culture. The well-preserved remains, rich history and stunning environment make it one of the most popular tourist destinations in Italy. Whether you're a history geek, an archaeology fanatic, or simply a lover of all things ancient, Pompeii is a location that will not disappoint.

Best Places of Accommodation to stay in Pompeii

Here are some of the greatest places to stay in Pompeii:

Grand Hotel Pompei: This hotel is located right in the heart of Pompeii, and provides guests with magnificent rooms, a spa, and an outdoor pool.

Villa Dei Misteri: This exquisite hotel is built in a restored 19th-century villa, and allows guests the option to see the magnificence of Pompeii in a more traditional environment.

Hotel Villa Dei Platani: This hotel is located in the countryside near Pompeii, and gives guests a calm getaway from the rush and bustle of the city, with modern rooms and a pool.

Pompeii B&Bs: For those looking for a more economical option, this bed and breakfast offers pleasant accommodations in a central location, making it a good choice for budget-conscious guests.

No matter the choice you choose, you're sure to have a delightful day seeing the interesting history and breathtaking remains of Pompeii.

Mount Vesuvius

Mount Vesuvius is a stratovolcano located in the Gulf of Naples in Italy. It is well known for its devastating eruption in 79 AD that devastated the Roman cities of Pompeii, Herculaneum, Stabiae, and Oplontis. The eruption was one of the most famous and catastrophic volcanic eruptions in history, burying these cities and their populations under a thick layer of ash and pumice.

Mount Vesuvius has a complex geological history, with multiple eruptions happening throughout its long history. The most famous of these eruptions was the one that took place in 79 AD, which was reported by Pliny the Younger in letters to the Roman historian Tacitus. Pliny, who was staying in Misenum at the time of the eruption, wrote that a vast cloud of ash and pumice rose into the sky, followed by a rain of ash and hot pebbles. The ash and pumice that fell from the sky buried the adjacent cities, preserving them in their original state until their rediscovery in the 16th and 17th centuries.

Today, Mount Vesuvius is a popular tourist site, attracting millions of visitors each year. The most popular destination is the archaeological site of Pompeii, where visitors may stroll through the ruins of the old city and witness the well-preserved remnants of buildings, streets, and public squares. Visitors can also explore the ruins of Herculaneum, Stabiae, and Oplontis, as well as the Vesuvian Villas, which are a group of well-preserved Roman villas located close to the volcano.

In addition to the archaeological sites, Mount Vesuvius offers various attractions for travelers. The mountain itself is a popular hiking destination, with various trails reaching the peak. At the summit, tourists can enjoy beautiful views of the surrounding landscape and the Gulf of Naples. There is also a tourist center at the summit, which gives information about the history and geology of the volcano, as well as a cafe and gift store.

Visitors to Mount Vesuvius should be prepared for a tough climb, as the trails to the summit are steep and rocky. It is recommended that visitors wear sturdy shoes and bring lots of drinks, as well as a hat and sunscreen. The routes to the top can be very congested during the peak tourist season, so visitors may prefer to arrive early or plan to visit during off-peak times.

Another favorite activity in the area is taking a beautiful drive down the Vesuvian Coast, which gives stunning views of the Gulf of Naples and the surrounding countryside. There are various settlements along the coast that provide a range of attractions, including historic ruins, medieval castles, and picturesque fishing villages.

In conclusion, Mount Vesuvius is a must-visit location for anyone interested in history, geology, or archaeology. With its well-preserved ancient ruins, spectacular views, and strenuous hikes, there is something for everyone at this legendary volcano. Whether you are a history buff, an outdoor enthusiast, or simply someone who loves seeing new and exciting locations, Mount Vesuvius is a destination that is sure to leave a lasting impact.

Best Places of Accommodation to stay in Mount Vesuvius

There are various possibilities for accommodation in the area, including:

Hotels: There are various hotels located in the towns surrounding Mount Vesuvius, such as Pompeii, Herculaneum, and Naples. These hotels range from budget-friendly options to luxury resorts.

Bed & Breakfasts: Bed and breakfasts are a popular alternative for individuals who desire a more private and homely experience. Many B&Bs are housed in old structures and offer spectacular views of the volcano and the surrounding surroundings.

Vacation Rentals: Vacation rentals such as apartments, villas, and houses are terrific alternatives for those traveling in bigger groups or families. These rentals offer more privacy and space than a hotel room, and many come with a kitchen, allowing you to save money on meals.

Camping Spots: For those who want a more rugged experience, there are various camping sites available around Mount Vesuvius. These attractions offer a unique opportunity to enjoy the area and its natural beauty.

When picking a place to stay, consider your budget, the size of your group, and your desired style of lodging. Additionally, bear in mind that many of the towns surrounding Mount Vesuvius can get congested during peak tourist season, so be sure to reserve in advance.

Castello Aragonese

Castello Aragonese is a historical castle located on the island of Ischia, off the coast of Naples, Italy. The castle was built in 474 BC by Hiero I of Syracuse and has been used as a military stronghold, a jail, and a palace over the years. It has been fully repaired and is now open to the public as a tourist attraction.

The castle is situated on a small island connected to the main island of Ischia by a bridge. The castle's location gives superb views of the surrounding area, including the Bay of Naples, the city of Naples, and Mount Vesuvius. Visitors can also see the ruins of the ancient Roman aqueduct that formerly brought water to the castle.

The castle's walls are composed of massive stone blocks and are up to 15 meters high in some areas. The walls are punctured by various towers, notably the Torre Dei Cannoni, which was used to defend the castle from invasions. The castle also has a chapel, several subterranean cisterns, and several residential buildings that were utilized by the castle's residents.

Visitors can explore the castle's ramparts, towers, and underground cisterns on a guided tour. They can also visit the castle's church, which has been wonderfully repaired and houses various holy objects. In addition, visitors can learn about the castle's history through displays and exhibitions that are positioned around the castle.

The castle's history is an interesting one. It was built around 474 BC by Hiero I of Syracuse and was utilized as a military stronghold for several decades. During the Roman period, the castle was utilized as a jail, and some renowned convicts were incarcerated there. In the Middle Ages, the castle was used as a residence by the Aragonese royal family.

In the 16th century, the castle was assaulted and seized by the French, who used it as a base from which to launch attacks on the surrounding area. The castle was eventually returned to the Aragonese, who used it as a residence until the 19th century.

Today, Castello Aragonese is a major tourist attraction, and visitors come from all over the world to see its gorgeous architecture, historic significance, and stunning views. The castle is open to the public year-round, and visitors can join guided tours or explore the castle on their own.

Castello Aragonese is a must-visit destination for anybody interested in history, architecture, and beautiful views. Its rich history, amazing architecture, and spectacular views make it a really unique and remarkable destination. Whether you're a history enthusiast, an architecture lover, or just someone searching for a lovely spot to visit, Castello Aragonese is sure to impress.

Best Places of Accommodation to stay near Castello Aragonese

Castello Aragonese provides many hotel alternatives available for travelers. Here are some of the top places to stay in Castello Aragonese:

Hotel Il Castello: This hotel offers spectacular views of Ischia Island and the Tyrrhenian Sea.

Terme Manzi Hotel & Spa: This hotel is a historic spa resort that boasts a large thermal pool and a variety of therapies. It offers nice rooms and apartments with sea views.

Albergo Il Monastero: This hotel is located in a former monastery and provides exquisite rooms with antique furnishings and stunning views of the sea.

These are some of the best places to stay in Castello Aragonese, offering a range of alternatives from luxury spa resorts to budget-friendly hotels. Visitors can choose the best lodging that meets their needs, budget, and preferences.

Marina Grande Beach

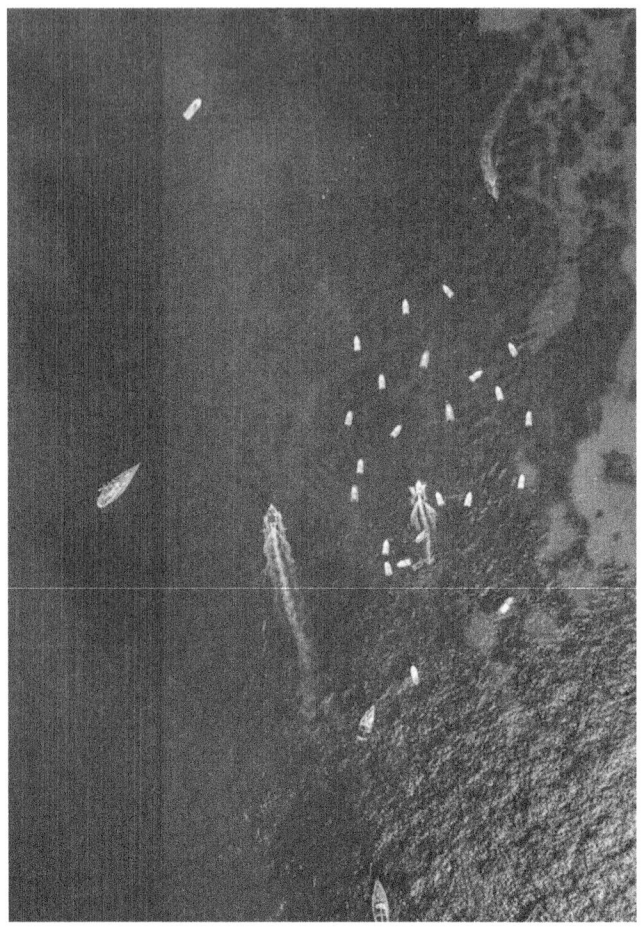

Marina Grande Beach is one of the most famous and beautiful beaches in the world. Located in the town of Sorrento on the Amalfi Coast in Italy, this beach is a popular destination for travelers from all over the world.

The beach is easily accessible and is located just a few minutes' walk from the center of Sorrento. Visitors can either take a bus from Sorrento or a ferry from the nearby town of Naples to get to Marina Grande Beach. Once there, guests will be welcomed by a breathtaking view of the crystal-clear waters of the Mediterranean and the lush green cliffs that surround the beach.

The sand on Marina Grande Beach is soft and golden, and the beach is lined with colorful umbrellas and loungers, making it the perfect place to relax and soak up the sun. The water is warm and very clear, and there are various spots where guests can swim, snorkel, and enjoy other water activities.

Marina Grande Beach is also recognized for its dynamic and boisterous vibe. There are various restaurants, cafes, and bars along the beach, and many of them offer outdoor dining with views of the sea. Visitors can have a tasty meal or a refreshing drink while taking in the breathtaking views of the Amalfi Coast.

For those who want to see the splendor of the Amalfi Coast from the water, there are various boat cruises accessible from Marina Grande Beach. These cruises allow visitors to appreciate the gorgeous coastline and visit some of the neighboring islands and bays. Some of the most popular boat cruises include journeys to the famous Blue Grotto, a sea cave that is lit by beautiful blue light, and the island of Capri, which is recognized for its spectacular natural beauty and luxury mansions.

One of the delights of Marina Grande Beach is the opportunity to observe the traditional fishing boats that are still utilized by the local fisherman. These boats, known as "gozzi," are brilliantly colored and are an iconic symbol of the Amalfi Coast. Visitors may see the fishermen bringing in their catch each day, and they can even purchase fresh seafood to savor at one of the local restaurants.

This Beach is also surrounded by various historic structures and monuments. Visitors can take a short stroll from the beach to visit the old Roman ruins of Sorrento, or they can climb the steps to the top of the hill to admire the spectacular views of the town and the sea. There are also other churches and monasteries in the vicinity that are worth seeing, including the famed Church of Santa Maria degli Angeli.

Finally, for those who want to experience the traditional culture and way of life of the Amalfi Coast, there are various local markets and festivals that take place in Sorrento and the surrounding area. These events are a terrific way to try local foods, see traditional crafts, and enjoy live music and dancing.

Marina Grande Beach is a must-visit place for everyone who is traveling to the Amalfi Coast. With its gorgeous natural environment, dynamic atmosphere, and rich cultural legacy, it is no wonder that this beach is one of the most popular places in Italy. Whether you are wanting to relax on the beach, enjoy water sports, or explore the history and culture of the region, Marina Grande Beach has something to offer everyone.

Best Places of Accommodation to stay in Marina Grande Beach

The following are some of the top locations to stay in Marina Grande Beach for a comprehensive tourist experience:

Grand Hotel Cocumella: This 5-star luxury hotel offers spectacular views of the sea, elegant rooms and suites, a private beach, and a gourmet restaurant.

Sorrento Palace Hotel: This 4-star hotel includes pleasant rooms and suites, a swimming pool, a terrace with views of the sea, and a restaurant serving local cuisine.

La Pergola Hotel: This 3-star hotel offers pleasant rooms, a patio with sea views, a swimming pool, and a restaurant serving classic Italian cuisine.

Hotel Royal Continental: This 4-star hotel has spacious rooms and suites, a private beach, a swimming pool, and a restaurant serving international cuisine.

Regardless of the hotel you choose, you'll be able to experience the magnificent splendor of Marina Grande

Beach and all the wonderful things that Sorrento has to offer.

Villa Rufolo

Mansion Rufolo is a medieval villa located in the center of Ravello, Italy, on the Amalfi Coast. This gorgeous and well-preserved edifice goes back to the 13th century and is a remarkable example of the Italian medieval architecture of that period. The house has a rich history and has been visited by many prominent people over the years.

The house was initially erected by the Rufolo family, one of the most important and affluent families in Ravello during the 13th century. Over the years, it has undergone various renovations and changes, although its original medieval structure and design have remained well-preserved. The estate boasts an outstanding tower, which offers stunning views of the Amalfi Coast and the

Mediterranean Sea, as well as a gorgeous garden with a central fountain, which is flanked by towering palm trees and colorful blossoms.

One of the most noteworthy aspects of Villa Rufolo is its gorgeous and ornate arched windows, which are embellished with elaborate carvings and stained glass. The interiors of the villa are similarly spectacular and contain high-vaulted ceilings, frescoed walls, and finely tiled flooring. The mansion also includes a spectacular music chamber, which is considered one of the most beautiful in the world and is utilized for concerts and events throughout the year.

The Villa Rufolo is also famed for its affiliation with Richard Wagner. Wagner was so captivated by the beauty of the villa and its garden that he selected it as the backdrop for his opera "Parsifal" second act. He characterized the mansion as "the most beautiful spot in the world," and it is thought that the villa and its garden were the primary sources of inspiration for the construction of the mythical kingdom of Klingsor in his opera.

The Villa Rufolo is currently open to the public and is a famous tourist destination in Ravello. Visitors can explore the villa and its grounds, see the breathtaking views from the tower, and attend concerts and activities in the music room. The garden of Villa Rufolo is also a favorite site for weddings and other special events, and its beauty has inspired many poets and painters throughout the years.

In addition to its rich history and beauty, Villa Rufolo is also noted for its cultural events and festivals. Every year, the Ravello Festival is hosted in the villa, and it is regarded as one of the most important cultural events in Italy. The festival comprises classical music concerts, opera performances, and other cultural events, and attracts tourists from all over the world.

Villa Rufolo is a particularly remarkable property that offers tourists a glimpse into the rich history and beauty of Italian medieval architecture. Its relationship with Richard Wagner and its use as the backdrop for his opera "Parsifal" has made it an even more important cultural destination, and its lovely garden and spectacular vistas make it a must-visit for everyone visiting the Amalfi Coast. Whether you're interested in history, culture, or just breathtaking vistas, Villa Rufolo is a location that you won't want to miss.

Best Places of Accommodation to stay in Villa Rufolo

If you're wanting to stay in the neighborhood, here are some popular hotel options:

Home Maria Ravello - A luxury hotel built in a renovated 19th-century villa with breathtaking views of the coast.

Hotel Caruso Ravello - A five-star hotel set in a former 11th-century palace with a rooftop terrace with views of the coast.

Palazzo Sasso - A premium hotel built in a restored 19th-century mansion with a rooftop patio, infinity pool, and sea views.

All of these lodgings are located close to Villa Rufolo and offer exceptional amenities and spectacular views of the Amalfi Coast. Choose the one that best meets your budget and tastes for a wonderful stay in the neighborhood.

Amalfi

Amalfi is a lovely coastal town located in the region of Campania. It is situated along the Amalfi Coast. The town is bordered by towering cliffs, crystal clear lakes, and lush foliage, which makes it a favorite destination for travelers from all over the world. Here's a detailed guide for travelers visiting Amalfi.

History and Culture:
Amalfi was originally a great maritime republic during the 11th century, and its past is evident in the many antique structures and monuments that still survive in the town today. The town is rich in culture, with a significant artistic and architectural legacy, including several antique churches, monasteries, and historical structures. One of the most notable structures in the

town is the Cathedral of St. Andrew, which is a classic example of Arab-Norman architecture and a must-visit for history and architecture fans.

Beaches:
The Amalfi Coast is known for its stunning beaches, and Amalfi is no exception. The town boasts several lovely beaches that are great for swimming, sunbathing, and relaxing. The most popular beach in Amalfi is Marina Grande Beach, another popular beach is the little cove of Atrani Beach, which is recognized for its pristine seas and attractive surroundings.

Food and Wine:
Amalfi is recognized for its exquisite native cuisine, which is focused on fresh seafood, olive oil, and herbs. Some of the must-try delicacies include spaghetti alle vongole (spaghetti with clams), scialatielli ai frutti di mare (fresh seafood pasta), and limoncello, a traditional lemon liqueur that is manufactured in the region. In addition to its meals, Amalfi is also famed for its wines, which are produced in the neighboring hills. Tourists can visit local wineries and vineyards to sample the local wines and learn more about the wine-making process.

Shopping:
Amalfi is an excellent area for shopping, with a wide range of local stores and boutiques that sell a variety of souvenirs and local products. Some of the most popular goods to buy include hand-painted ceramics, handmade paper products, and classic lemon-scented soaps and

lotions. There are also various local markets where tourists can buy fresh produce, fish, and local handicrafts.

Outdoor Activities:
Amalfi is an excellent site for outdoor sports, with a wide range of chances for hiking, sailing, kayaking, and more. The Amalfi Coast is famous for its lovely coastal walks, with various routes that give breathtaking views of the surrounding hills and sea. For those who prefer sailing, there are various boat tours that offer scenic trips along the coast and to the nearby islands. Kayaking is also a popular pastime, with various rental firms offering kayaks for tourists to explore the magnificent coastline.

Amalfi is a lovely coastal town that offers something for everyone. From its rich history and culture to its lovely beaches and wonderful cuisine, there is always something to see and do in this picturesque corner of Italy. Whether you are a history lover, a foodie, or just seeking for a tranquil escape, Amalfi is the perfect destination for your next holiday.

Best Places of Accommodation to stay in Amalfi

There are several hotel alternatives available to meet different interests and budgets. Here are some of the greatest places to stay in Amalfi:

There are various hotels in Amalfi that offer varying levels of comfort, from luxury to budget-friendly. Some popular options include Hotel Santa Caterina, Hotel Luna Convento, and Hotel Marina Riviera.

Regardless of where you stay in Amalfi, you're guaranteed to appreciate the town's rich history, breathtaking coastline, and wonderful cuisine.

Salerno

Salerno is a city located on the southwestern coast of the Campania region. It is noted for its rich history, magnificent natural beauty, and thriving cultural environment. It is a popular location for travelers from across the world and offers a wide choice of activities and attractions for visitors to enjoy.

One of the most prominent landmarks in Salerno is the Castello di Arechi, a medieval castle that was built in the 9th century. The castle offers excellent views of the city and the surrounding countryside and is a popular site for tourists to visit. Another renowned site is the Cathedral of Salerno, a stunning building that was built in the 11th century. The cathedral has a mix of architectural styles, including Romanesque and Gothic, and is a must-visit for anybody interested in religious history and architecture.

The Amalfi Coast is just a short drive from Salerno. The coast is also home to several prominent beaches, including the famed Praiano, where visitors can relax and soak up the sun. There are also various environmental reserves and parks in the vicinity, including the Parco Naturale Regionale di Valle dell'Inferno e Bussento, which allows visitors the opportunity to stroll and explore the local flora and wildlife.

Another must-visit sight in Salerno is the Museo Archeologico Provinciale, which houses a variety of relics from the city's rich history, including Roman mosaics, Etruscan ceramics, and Greek vases. The museum also allows visitors the opportunity to learn about the history of Salerno and the surrounding area, especially its role as a major center of study and medical during the medieval period.

Salerno is also known for its rich cultural scene, with a large selection of events and festivals taking place throughout the year. Some of the most prominent events include the Salerno Film Festival, the Salerno International Poetry Prize, and the Salerno Jazz Festival. The city is also home to various theaters, including the Teatro Verdi and the Teatro Augusteo, which stage a variety of shows throughout the year.

When it comes to food, Salerno is a foodie's dream, with a vast choice of local specialties to taste. Some of the most famous meals in the area include seafood dishes like spaghetti alle vongole (spaghetti with clams) and fritto misto (mixed fried seafood), as well as pizza and pasta dishes created with local ingredients like mozzarella di bufala and San Marzano tomatoes. Visitors can also enjoy some of the local wines, including the famed DOC Costiera Amalfitana wine.

Salerno is a city that provides something for everyone, from its rich history and magnificent natural beauty to its bustling cultural scene and superb local cuisine. Whether you are interested in history, nature, culture, or gastronomy, Salerno has plenty to offer, making it a must-visit destination for travelers from around the world.

Best Places of Accommodation to stay in Salerno

When it comes to accommodations, there are various options to select from, ranging from luxury hotels to budget-friendly options. Here are some of the top places to stay in Salerno:

Grand Hotel Salerno: This is a luxury hotel located in the center of Salerno, with magnificent accommodations, top-notch services, and breathtaking views of the Mediterranean.

Plaza Hotel: This is a four-star hotel located in the city center, offering nice accommodations, an outdoor pool, and convenient access to local attractions.

No matter what your budget or preferences are, you are sure to discover the right location to stay in Salerno.

Piazza del Municipio

Piazza del Municipio is a square located in Naples and is noted for its historical and cultural significance. The square is situated in the middle of the city and acts as a focal point for tourism and local activities. It is flanked by several prominent buildings, including the City Hall, Castel dell'Ovo, and the Royal Palace of Naples.

City Hall, also known as the Palazzo del Municipio, is located on the east side of the square and serves as the seat of the local administration. It was erected in the 19th century in the Neoclassical style and is one of the largest buildings in the square. The structure is highlighted by its large entrance, majestic columns, and beautiful sculptures.

Castel dell'Ovo is a castle located on an island in the bay of Naples, and it is one of the city's most famous sights. The castle goes back to the Roman period and has served as a military fortification, prison, and royal residence throughout its history. Today, it is a museum and is open to visitors who want to discover its rich history and spectacular views of the city.

The Royal Palace of Naples is located on the west side of the plaza and was the royal residence of the Bourbon family in the 18th and 19th centuries. It is now a museum open to the public. Visitors can tour the spectacular interior, which is packed with exquisite furnishings, beautiful decorations, and stunning artwork.

In addition to its historical and cultural value, Piazza del Municipio is also a popular gathering spot for locals and tourists alike. The square is surrounded by cafés and restaurants, making it a great place to relax and have a meal or drink while taking in the views and sounds of the city. The square also contains a big fountain, which provides a quiet backdrop for people to relax and converse or simply enjoy the vista.

The square is also a popular venue for events and festivals. Throughout the year, the square is utilized for concerts, parades, and other events, which attract enormous groups of people. These events are a terrific chance to see the city's unique culture and see the square come to life with enthusiasm and energy.

Piazza del Municipio is an essential destination for everyone visiting Naples. The area is a symbol of the city's rich history and culture, and it acts as a focal focus for tourism and local events. Whether you are interested in discovering the city's stunning architecture, experiencing its colorful culture, or simply enjoying a meal or drink in the sun, Piazza del Municipio is the perfect site to start your tour.

Overall, the Amalfi Coast offers a unique blend of natural beauty, and rich history that is likely to capture and delight visitors.

Best Places of Accommodation to stay in Piazza del Municipio

Some of the top places to stay in the area include:

Grand Hotel Parker's: This is a 5-star hotel located in the center of Naples. It features magnificent accommodations, a rooftop patio with views of the bay, and a fine dining restaurant.

La Ciliegina Lifestyle Hotel: This is a boutique hotel located in the historical center of Naples. It provides exquisite accommodations, a rooftop patio with views of the city, and a restaurant serving classic Neapolitan cuisine.

Palazzo Alabardieri: This is a 4-star hotel housed in a restored 19th-century building near Piazza del Municipio. It features spacious rooms, a rooftop patio, and a bar serving aperitifs and cocktails.

Starhotels Terminus: This is a 4-star hotel located near Piazza del Municipio and the central railway station. It features nice accommodations, a fitness facility, and a restaurant providing foreign cuisine.

These are just a few of the many alternatives accessible in the Piazza del Municipio region. It's advisable to read internet reviews and compare costs to discover the best lodging that meets your demands and budget.

Top Italian Cuisine to Try Out

The cuisine of the Amalfi Coast is a reflection of its distinct history and geography, boasting fresh seafood, fragrant herbs and spices, and local products.

Some popular Dishes and Drinks Include:

Limoncello

Limoncello is a lemon-flavored liquor that is often created locally. It is prepared from the zest of Sorrento lemons, which are noted for their peculiar and delicious aroma. The traditional process of creating Limoncello requires steeping the lemon zest in high-proof alcohol, such as Everclear, for several days to extract the flavor and aroma. The alcohol is then blended with a simple syrup prepared from water and sugar, resulting in a sweet and tangy liqueur with a bright yellow color.

Limoncello is a popular drink for visitors visiting the Amalfi Coast and other parts of Southern Italy, where it is typically served as a digestive after meals. It is also used in a number of cocktails and pastries. In recent years, Limoncello has gained famous in various areas of the world and is now made in many nations outside of Italy.

Visitors to the Amalfi Coast can sometimes take tours of Limoncello distilleries, where they can learn about the history and production process of this famous Italian liqueur. Tasting rooms are also a popular component of these distilleries, letting tourists try several varieties of Limoncello and purchase bottles to take home as mementos.

This drink has a distinctive and tasty drink that is closely related to the culture and history of Southern Italy. Whether sipped as a digestif or incorporated in cocktails, it is a must-try for tourists visiting the region.

Pizza Margherita

Pizza Margherita is a typical Neapolitan pizza that is widely considered to be one of the best examples of traditional Italian food. The meal is produced with basic and fresh ingredients that are combined to create a flavor explosion on your tongue. Here is a detailed description of Pizza Margherita for tourists:

The base of a Margherita pizza is a simple dough composed of flour, yeast, water, and salt. This is then topped with a tomato sauce made from canned or fresh San Marzano tomatoes, mozzarella cheese, and fresh basil leaves. Some varieties may additionally contain a drizzle of extra-virgin olive oil.

Pizza Margherita is supposed to have been invented in honor of Queen Margherita of Savoy in the late 19th century. The colors of the pizza, red (tomato sauce), white (mozzarella cheese), and green (basil leaves), were chosen to mimic the colors of the Italian flag. The dish immediately grew famous and is now widely regarded as an icon of Italian cuisine.

To prepare a Pizza Margherita, the dough is first flattened out into a thin, round form. The tomato sauce is then distributed evenly over the dough, allowing a little space around the borders for the crust. The mozzarella cheese is then put on top of the sauce, followed by a handful of fresh basil leaves. The pizza is then roasted in a wood-fired oven at a high temperature (450°C - 500°C) for around 90 seconds to 2 minutes until the crust is crispy and the cheese is melted.

Pizza Margherita is often served hot and fresh from the oven, sliced into slices, and enjoyed as an entree or a snack. It is also common to complement the dish with a glass of red wine or a cold beer. This Pizza is commonly regarded as a classic and conventional pizza, however, there are various versions of the meal that have been made throughout the years. Some of the most common varieties include the addition of various toppings, such as olives, mushrooms, onions, and peppers, to make a more savory and diverse pizza.

Pizza Margherita can be found at many Italian restaurants and pizzerias around the world. However, the ideal spot to try this meal is in its birthplace, Naples, Italy. Here, you will discover several historic pizzerias that have been making this dish for centuries and have perfected the technique of making a genuine Margherita pizza.

When ordering a Pizza Margherita, it is crucial to note that excellent ingredients are key to the dish's success. Look for pizzerias that use fresh and high-quality mozzarella cheese, San Marzano tomatoes, and basil leaves. Also, be sure to try the pizza hot from the oven for the finest experience.

Pizza Margherita is a traditional dish that is a must-try for everyone who loves pizza or Italian food. With its simple and fresh ingredients, it is a monument to the power of simplicity and how a few simple elements can come together to make a genuinely delightful dish. Whether you're in Italy or anywhere else in the world, be sure to give Pizza Margherita a try and enjoy the taste of tradition and the enchantment of Italian cuisine.

Seafood pasta

Shellfish pasta Margherita is a popular Italian meal that mixes the fresh aromas of seafood with the acidic and bright taste of a Margherita pizza. The dish consists of pasta, often spaghetti or linguine that is paired with a sauce made from fresh tomatoes, garlic, basil, and olive oil. To this sauce, a range of shellfish is added, including shrimp, mussels, clams, and sometimes scallops or squid. The end product is a tasty and flavorful dinner that is both filling and fulfilling.

One of the important ingredients in seafood pasta Margherita is sauce. To make this sauce, you will need ripe and juicy tomatoes. It is vital to use the freshest and ripest tomatoes available since they will add the greatest flavor and sweetness to the sauce. The tomatoes are first peeled and seeded, and then they are sliced into little pieces. In a large saucepan, the chopped tomatoes are blended with minced garlic, fresh basil leaves, and extra-virgin olive oil. The sauce is then simmered over medium heat until the flavors have melted together and the sauce has thickened somewhat.

The seafood that is used in seafood spaghetti Margherita is a significant aspect of the dish, and it is normally chosen based on personal liking and what is available at the time. Some of the most common types of seafood used in this dish include shrimp, mussels, clams, and scallops. The seafood is washed and readied, and then it is sautéed in a separate pan until it is fully done. The fish is then added to the tomato sauce, and the meal is heated through until the flavors have melted together.

When it comes to preparing pasta, it is vital to choose pasta that will hold up well in the sauce. Spaghetti and linguine are both popular choices for this dish, as they are robust enough to hold up to the sauce without getting soggy. The pasta is cooked according to package directions, and then it is drained and added to the seafood and tomato sauce. The pasta is tossed with the sauce, and the meal is heated through until the pasta is well coated and the flavors have melted together.

The finished meal is generally served with freshly grated Parmesan cheese and extra basil leaves. The dish is then served hot and quickly relished. The tastes of the fresh tomato sauce, the garlicky shellfish, and the al dente pasta all come together in a delicious and gratifying way. The recipe is both savory and full, making it a great choice for a complete meal.

Seafood spaghetti Margherita is a classic Italian meal that is both tasty and easy to create. The recipe mixes the fresh flavors of seafood with the tangy and bright taste of a Margherita pizza, resulting in a tasty and substantial dinner that is sure to satisfy. Whether you are a seasoned cook or a beginner, this dish is sure to impress, and it is a terrific way to savor the taste of Italy from the comfort of your own home.

Mozzarella di Bufala

Mozzarella di Bufala, often known as buffalo mozzarella, is a type of cheese prepared from the milk of the indigenous Italian water buffalo. It is considered to be one of the most famous and traditional cheeses in Italy, with a long and rich history reaching back to the 9th century.

It is produced largely in the areas of Campania, Lazio, and Puglia, and is created by hand using a traditional method that involves boiling and stretching the curd to create a soft and creamy texture. The milk used to manufacture this cheese is high in fat and protein, which gives it its particular flavor and texture.

One of the primary aspects of Mozzarella di Bufala is its delicate and creamy texture. When fresh, it is soft, juicy, and has a somewhat sour taste. The cheese is also noted for its delicate and subtle flavor, which is significantly milder than the taste of cow's milk mozzarella.

Mozzarella di Bufala is extensively used in a variety of recipes, including pizza, Caprese salad, and spaghetti. It is also a favorite cheese for snacking and is commonly served with fresh tomatoes, basil, and balsamic vinegar.

It is also a protected food product in Europe, with the EU awarding it the designation of "protected designation of origin" (PDO) in 1996. This means that only cheese produced in specified regions of Italy and manufactured with traditional methods can be labeled as "Mozzarella di Bufala." This classification aims to protect the originality and quality of the cheese, ensuring that only the best and most authentic products are offered to consumers.

To assure the quality of Mozzarella di Bufala, it is vital to obtain the cheese from a trustworthy supplier and to search for the PDO label on the container. When stored carefully, the cheese will stay fresh for up to a week, and it should be enjoyed as soon as possible after purchase for the greatest flavor and texture.

Mozzarella di Bufala is a traditional and authentic Italian cheese with a long history and a unique flavor and texture. It is extensively used in a variety of cuisines and is a favorite cheese for snacking. With its protected designation of origin, consumers can be guaranteed that they are obtaining a high-quality and original product. Whether you are a gourmand or a cheese enthusiast, Mozzarella di Bufala is definitely worth experiencing on your next vacation to Italy.

Italian Fried Seafood Platter

The Italian fried seafood platter is a dish that contains a range of seafood dishes that are battered and deep-fried to golden perfection. This platter often includes a mix of seafood products such as calamari, shrimp, scallops, and white fish, but can also include other seafood dishes such as crab cakes or clams.

The batter used for the Italian fried seafood plate is often a blend of flour, cornstarch, baking powder, and spices. This provides a light and crispy covering that perfectly encases the luscious and delicate seafood inside. The seafood is first dredged in the batter, then gently dropped into hot oil to fry till golden brown.

One of the crucial aspects of the success of this dish is the quality of the fish used. Fresh and high-quality seafood is vital to making a delightful and delectable plate. The seafood should be cleaned and prepped correctly, then battered and fried right before serving to ensure the finest possible taste and texture.

Once the seafood is cooked, it is normally rinsed on paper towels to remove any extra oil. The platter is then presented on a big serving plate, frequently accompanied by a choice of dipping sauces, such as tartar sauce, cocktail sauce, or a lemon-butter sauce.

The Italian fried seafood platter is a popular dish at many Italian restaurants, especially those that specialize in seafood. This dish is commonly served as a starter or as a main course and may be appreciated by both seafood aficionados and those who are just searching for a good and satisfying dinner.

In addition to its wonderful taste, the Italian fried seafood platter is also an aesthetically stunning dish. The golden brown batter and the colorful assortment of seafood ingredients make for a magnificent appearance that is guaranteed to impress.

When dining out, it is crucial to find a restaurant that is well renowned for its seafood and has a reputation for offering high-quality, fresh seafood. This will ensure that you are enjoying the finest possible Italian fried seafood platter experience.

The Italian fried seafood platter is a wonderful and gratifying dish that is guaranteed to please both seafood fans and those looking for a delicious supper. With its crispy batter, succulent and delicate seafood, and spectacular presentation, this dish is a must-try for everyone visiting Italy. Whether served as a starter or as a main dish, the Italian fried seafood platter is sure to be a wonderful dining experience that you will not soon forget.

Almond granita

Almond granita is a type of Italian frozen dessert made from sugar, water, and almonds. It is comparable in texture to sorbet but has a more grainy, crunchy texture due to the manner it is created.

To prepare almond granita, the ingredients are mixed and then frozen in shallow pans. As the mixture begins to freeze, it is scraped and mixed constantly to achieve a crisp texture. This technique is performed multiple times until the mixture reaches the desired consistency.

The flavor of almond granita is sweet and nutty, with a pronounced almond scent. The almonds used in the recipe can be either whole or ground, however, it is recommended to use high-quality, natural almonds to enhance the flavor. Some recipes also call for the use of lemon zest or almond extract to further improve the flavor.

In Italy, almond granita is often eaten as a pleasant summer treat, especially in the coastal districts of Sicily where it is thought to have originated. It is generally served in a tall glass with a dab of whipped cream on top.

The versatility of almond granita makes it a popular choice for people looking for a sweet, refreshing dessert. It can be eaten on its own as a treat or as a topping for ice cream or cake. It can also be used as a foundation for cocktails or as a refreshing addition to breakfast smoothies.

One of the advantages of almond granita is its simplicity. Unlike other frozen desserts, it requires no special equipment or ingredients, making it easy to cook at home. Additionally, it can be made in advance and stored in the freezer for later use.

Almond granita is a tasty and adaptable frozen treat that is great for people searching for a refreshing and fulfilling dessert. Its unusual texture, sweet and nutty flavor and ease of preparation make it a popular choice for people searching for a simple yet fulfilling dessert. Whether savored on its own or used as a topping for other delicacies, almond granita is a must-try for anyone who adores frozen desserts.

Sfogliatella pastry

Sfogliatella is a type of pastry that is specific to the Italian province of Campania. It is considered a classic Neapolitan pastry, and it is a popular delicacy for tourists visiting the region. The term "sfogliatella" means "small leaf" in Italian, which is a reference to the pastry's layered, flaky structure.

The pastry is prepared with a thick, buttery dough that is rolled and folded to produce numerous layers. The dough is then filled with a sweet mixture of ricotta cheese, sugar, lemon zest, and candied orange peel. The filled dough is then molded into a crescent moon or shell shape and cooked till golden brown.

Sfogliatella comes in two main varieties: "sfogliatella riccia" and "sfogliatella frolla." Sfogliatella riccia is produced with a more layered and flaky dough, whereas sfogliatella frolla has a more cookie-like texture. Both types are equally excellent and are enjoyed by locals and visitors alike.

It can be found in pastry shops and bakeries throughout the Campania area, as well as in other parts of Italy. It is commonly served as a dessert or a sweet snack, and it is also a popular dish to take on the go. Many people love it with a cup of espresso or cappuccino, as the sweetness of the pastry mixes nicely with the harshness of the coffee.

In addition to being a delightful delicacy, it is also a part of the cultural history of the Campania area. The pastry has a lengthy history, and it is thought to have been made by monks in the 16th century. Over the decades, it has become a mainstay of Neapolitan cuisine, and it is a favorite pastry among locals and tourists alike.

For tourists visiting Campania, trying sfogliatella is a must. Not only is it a tasty treat, but it is also a means to experience the local culture and food. Many pastry shops and bakeries in the region offer it prepared fresh every day, and they are always delighted to share the history and tradition behind this cherished treat.

When picking a sfogliatella, it is vital to search for a pastry that is flaky and golden brown in color.

Grilled octopus

Italian grilled octopus is a traditional meal that is popular in coastal areas of Italy. It's produced by grilling a full octopus over an open flame or hot coals until it's crispy on the outside and tender on the inside. The meal is often served as a main course and is often coupled with a fresh salad, crusty bread, and a glass of wine.

The key to preparing a perfect grilled octopus is to start with high-quality, fresh octopus. Ideally, it should be caught the same day that you plan to cook it. When selecting an octopus, opt for one that is firm to the touch, with a purplish-blue color, and without any strong scents. If the octopus smells excessively fishy or has a mushy texture, it's best to avoid it.

Once you have a fresh octopus, the first step in preparing it is to clean and tenderize it. This entails cooking it in a huge pot of water with vinegar, salt, and other seasonings until it's soft and tender. After boiling, it's crucial to let the octopus cool to room temperature before grilling. This allows the flavors to thoroughly penetrate the meat, and the cool temperature prevents it from turning tough and rubbery when grilled.

Grilling the octopus is the final stage and is where the dish obtains its signature smokey taste. The octopus is seasoned with olive oil, salt, and other spices before being set over hot coals. It's vital to grill the octopus slowly, turning it occasionally until it's crispy on the exterior and delicate on the inside. The cooking time depends depend on the size of the octopus, but it normally takes approximately 10-15 minutes.

When the octopus is done, it's generally served with a simple salad of fresh greens, lemon juice, and olive oil. Some people also like to spray a little balsamic vinegar over the top, which provides a tangy sweetness that pairs nicely with the smokey flavor of the grilled octopus.

Italian grilled octopus is a wonderful and classic dish that is great for seafood lovers. It's a fantastic meal to enjoy on a nice summer day, either at a local seafood restaurant or at home on your own barbecue. Enjoy your Italian grilled octopus with a glass of crisp white wine, and you'll have a delightful and real Italian dining experience.

Caprese salad

Caprese salad is a typical Italian meal that consists of fresh mozzarella cheese, ripe tomatoes, and basil leaves, all stacked on top of each other and drizzled with olive oil and balsamic vinegar. The dish is said to have originated in the province of Campania in Italy and is named after the island of Capri. The dish is often served as an appetizer or as a light supper, and its simple ingredients and refreshing taste make it a popular choice for summer dining.

The primary elements of a Caprese salad are ripe tomatoes, fresh mozzarella cheese, and basil leaves. The tomatoes should be firm and juicy, with a vibrant red color and a sweet, delicious flavor. The mozzarella cheese should be manufactured from water buffalo milk, if feasible, as this form of cheese has a creamier and more delicate taste than mozzarella made from cow's milk. The basil leaves should be fresh and fragrant, with a bright green color and a strong, sweet flavor.

To make a classic Caprese salad, they start by slicing the tomatoes and mozzarella cheese into rounds about 1/4 inch thick. Alternately they layer the tomato and cheese rounds on a dish, making sure to overlap them slightly. Then, a basil leaf is inserted between each layer of cheese and tomato. Once the layers are complete, they drizzle the entire dish with a good grade of extra virgin olive oil and matured balsamic vinegar.

The olive oil and balsamic vinegar enhance the flavor of the cheese, tomatoes, and basil, and serve to bring all of the flavors together in a perfect balance. The oil adds richness and a nutty flavor, while the balsamic vinegar delivers a tangy sweetness that matches the sweetness of the tomatoes.

Caprese salad can be eaten as is, or it can be spiced up with a variety of various toppings. Some popular additions include:

Pesto: A mixture of basil, pine nuts, garlic, and olive oil, pesto gives an extra burst of flavor to the salad.

Prosciutto: Thinly sliced prosciutto, a cured Italian ham, provides a salty and savory contrast to the sweet and creamy cheese and tomatoes.

Avocado: Adding ripe avocado to the salad gives it a creamy texture and a nutty flavor.

Grilled or roasted veggies: Grilling or roasting vegetables like bell peppers, zucchini, or eggplant adds a smokey flavor and a crunchy texture to the salad.

Nuts: Adding a sprinkling of nuts like almonds, pistachios, or walnuts gives the salad a crunch and a nutty flavor.

It is a versatile dish that can be served as an appetizer, a side dish, or as a main course. When served as a main course, it can be paired with a fresh green salad, a crusty baguette, or a bowl of pasta. It is a fantastic dish for summertime, as it is light and refreshing, and can be cooked in advance and stored in the refrigerator until ready to serve.

Caprese salad is a popular Italian dish that is easy, fresh, and tasty. With its combination of ripe tomatoes, fresh mozzarella cheese, and basil leaves, it is a dish that is great for summer dining. Whether dressed up with toppings or served simply, a Caprese salad is a dish that will always be admired for its refreshing taste and gorgeous aesthetic.

Gelato

Gelato, often known as Italian ice cream, is a typical treat for tourists visiting the Amalfi Coast in Italy. Originating in the 16th century, gelato is a creamy and delectable dessert that has become famous all over the world for its unique flavor and texture.

One of the most popular pastimes for tourists visiting the Amalfi Coast is to try the local gelato, which is noted for its great quality and unique flavor.

One of the defining qualities of gelato is its creamy texture, which is produced by adding a larger proportion of milk compared to other forms of ice cream. This results in a lighter, smoother, and more refreshing delight that is excellent for enjoying on a hot day on the Amalfi Coast. The gelato is also often served at a slightly warmer temperature compared to other forms of ice cream, which enhances the flavor and makes it more fun to eat.

Another distinctive quality of gelato is its wide choice of flavors, which are inspired by local foods and customs. On the Amalfi Coast, you may buy gelato in a variety of flavors, including classic favorites such as vanilla, chocolate, and strawberry, as well as more exotic flavors like limoncello (a lemon-flavored liqueur), pistachio, and hazelnut. These flavors are prepared with actual ingredients, such as fresh fruit, nuts, and spices, which give the gelato its original taste and aroma.

Gelato is also known for its health benefits. Unlike other forms of ice cream, gelato includes fewer fat and calories, making it a healthier treat that can be enjoyed in moderation. Gelato is also a fantastic source of calcium, which is vital for maintaining strong bones and teeth.

For travelers visiting the Amalfi Coast, trying gelato is a must. There are many gelaterias (gelato businesses) sprinkled across the neighborhood, each offering its own distinct assortment of tastes. Whether you favor classic or exotic flavors, there is sure to be a gelateria that provides what you are searching for. Some of the top gelaterias on the Amalfi Coast are Sorbillo, and Grom, which are noted for their high-quality gelato and courteous service.

Gelato is an essential component of the Amalfi Coast experience for tourists. With its creamy texture, a vast selection of flavors, and health advantages, it is no wonder that this wonderful treat has grown so famous all over the world. Whether you are a fan of classic flavors or are seeking to try something new, the Amalfi Coast is the perfect destination to taste some of the best gelatos in Italy. So, if you are planning a trip to the Amalfi Coast, make sure to add gelato to your list of must-try experiences!

Grilled Eggplant

Grilled eggplant is a simple dish cooked with fresh, local vegetables and is a mainstay of the Mediterranean diet.

The eggplant used in this meal is often the long, slender kind known as the Italian eggplant. These eggplants are collected in the summer months when they are at their pinnacle of flavor. The eggplant is cut lengthwise and then roasted over hot coals until soft and slightly browned. The smokey flavor of the grill combined with the natural sweetness of the eggplant gives a delightful taste sensation.

Once grilled, the eggplant can be eaten as is or topped with a variety of toppings such as olive oil, fresh herbs, salt, and lemon juice. This dish is commonly enjoyed as an appetizer or a side dish, but can also be served as a main course when coupled with a variety of meats or cheeses. The simplicity of the meal allows the natural tastes of the eggplant to come through, making it a favorite choice among locals and visitors alike.

The Amalfi Coast is recognized for its vivid and savory food, with an emphasis on fresh, seasonal ingredients. Many of the foods offered in this area contain seafood, as the coast is home to a long fishing culture. Grilled eggplant is a flexible dish that can be enjoyed in a number of settings, from casual beachside cafés to fine dining places.

When visiting the Amalfi Coast, it is a necessity to eat some of the local specialties, including grilled eggplant. This dish is a terrific opportunity to sample the flavors of the region and to explore the culinary traditions of the area. Whether consumed as a light lunch or a hefty dinner, grilled eggplant is a delightful and comforting dish that is sure to become a favorite among visitors.

Grilled eggplant is a popular meal found along the Amalfi Coast in Italy that displays the region's fondness for fresh, seasonal vegetables. This simple dish is produced with locally grown eggplant and is grilled to perfection, offering a pleasant and tasty experience for all who try it. Whether enjoyed as an appetizer, side dish, or main course, grilled eggplant is a must-try for those visiting the Amalfi Coast and wishing to taste the region's cuisine.

Tomato and Basil bruschetta

Tomato and basil bruschetta is a typical Italian snack that is often enjoyed on the picturesque Amalfi Coast. The dish comprises slices of grilled bread that are topped with ripe tomatoes, fresh basil, olive oil, and sometimes a sprinkle of salt and pepper.

This region is particularly famed for its fresh ingredients, and the tomatoes used in bruschetta here are no exception. The mild Mediterranean climate of the Amalfi Coast gives the right circumstances for cultivating luscious, sweet tomatoes that are rich in flavor.

When it comes to the basil utilized in the meal, the Amalfi Coast is home to some of the best basil in Italy. This aromatic herb gives a touch of freshness to the dish and helps to balance out the acidity of the tomatoes. The basil is generally gathered fresh right before it is used, ensuring that the flavor is at its finest.

In terms of preparation, the dish is fairly simple to produce. The bread is often sliced from a larger loaf and then grilled until it is crisp and slightly browned. The slices are then topped with juicy slices of tomato, broken basil leaves, and a drizzle of high-quality olive oil. A sprinkle of salt and pepper can be added to taste, however, the dish is frequently enjoyed simply with just the bread, tomatoes, basil, and oil.

When it comes to eating tomato and basil bruschetta on the Amalfi Coast, there are numerous possibilities. The dish can be found on the menus of many local trattorias and ristorantes and is often served as an appetizer or a light snack. Alternatively, it can be easily produced at home using locally obtained products, making it a wonderful alternative for individuals who like to cook their own food while on vacation.

In terms of pairing, tomato and basil bruschetta is commonly served with a chilled glass of white wine or a delightful lemon-flavored sparkling water. This helps to balance out the flavors of the dish and adds a bit of refinement to the feast.

Aside from being tasty, tomato and basil bruschetta is also a terrific opportunity to experience the local culture and cuisine of the Amalfi Coast. This recipe is a fantastic example of the basic yet flavorsome food that is so prominent in this region and provides a glimpse into the Mediterranean way of life.

Tomato and basil bruschetta is a must-try dish for anybody visiting the Amalfi Coast. The combination of juicy tomatoes, aromatic basil, and crisp, grilled bread is the pinnacle of Mediterranean flavor and is guaranteed to be a success for anybody who enjoys fresh, tasty food. So next time you're on the Amalfi Coast, make sure to have a piece or two of this classic Italian meal and sample the local flavors for yourself.

Seafood Risotto

Seafood risotto is a popular dish on the Amalfi Coast, the recipe blends creamy arborio rice with a range of seafood items, resulting in a delicious and savory lunch.

The backbone of the seafood risotto is the rice, which is often cooked with onion, garlic, and white wine, creating a rich and savory foundation for the shellfish. Next, the seafood is added to the dish. This can incorporate a range of items, such as shrimp, mussels, scallops, squid, or clams. The shellfish are sautéed with the rice, which serves to infuse the dish with its deep, salty flavor.

One of the main factors of a perfect seafood risotto is the timing. The rice should be cooked just until it is al dente, with a creamy texture that is not too soft or too hard. The seafood should be added at the correct moment so that it is precisely cooked but not overdone. The outcome is a dish that is rich in flavor and texture, with each element complementing the others perfectly.

The Amalfi Coast is known for its bountiful fish, making it the perfect site to eat seafood risotto. The region is home to a variety of seafood, including shrimp, mussels, clams, and several species of fish. This fresh seafood is the secret to the exquisite flavor of the risotto since the local seafood produces a unique flavor that is not found elsewhere.

Another key ingredient of the seafood risotto in Amalfi Coast is the sauce. In many recipes, a tomato-based sauce is added to the dish, which helps to bring out the flavors of the shellfish and gives a balance between the rich, creamy rice and the saline seafood. Some varieties additionally add lemon or herbs such as basil or parsley, which lend a fresh and lively flavor to the dish.

When it comes to serving seafood risotto, there are several alternatives. Some restaurants serve it as a main course, while others offer it as an appetizer or as a side dish. Regardless of how it is prepared, the dish is guaranteed to be a favorite with seafood enthusiasts, since it is a full and tasty lunch that is sure to wow.

Seafood risotto is a popular and tasty meal in the Amalfi Coast, blending creamy arborio rice with a variety of seafood items. The secret to a perfect seafood risotto is time, as the rice and fish must be cooked exactly properly in order to make a pleasing and savory dish. With its bountiful fish and rich sauce, seafood risotto is a must-try for travelers visiting the Amalfi Coast, who are wanting to enjoy the exquisite cuisine of southern Italy.

Linguine with Clams

Linguine with clams is a favorite meal on the Amalfi Coast. Linguine is a form of pasta that is thin and flat and is produced with semolina flour and water. The pasta is often served with a light sauce, such as a tomato sauce or a seafood sauce, as it is in this recipe. Clams are a type of shellfish that are often used in numerous Italian recipes, including linguine with clams.

The recipe is produced by cooking the linguine pasta in boiling salted water until al dente, then draining and laying it aside. While the pasta is cooking, the clams are prepped by cleaning them and removing any sand or grit. The clams are then placed in a saucepan with some garlic, white wine, and olive oil, and cooked until they open.

The cooked clams and their cooking liquid are then added to the cooked linguine, along with some freshly cut parsley and lemon juice. The pasta is stirred together until the clams are uniformly distributed, and the sauce is softly coating the pasta. The dish is then served hot, with freshly grated Parmesan cheese on the side.

The tastes of linguine with clams are simple and fresh, with the taste of the sea from the clams, the light garlic and white wine, and the fresh parsley and lemon. The dish is light and tasty and is great for a sunny day on the Amalfi Coast.

The Amalfi Coast is famous for its seafood, and linguine with clams is a superb illustration of the region's cuisine. The clams used in the meal are usually native to the region and are recognized for their sweet, briny flavor. The pasta is also locally created and is customarily dried in the sun, giving it a particular flavor and texture.

Visitors to the Amalfi Coast can get this meal in many of the region's seafood restaurants, which are often located near the coast and offer a range of seafood dishes. These restaurants also generally offer a choice of local wines to compliment the dish, giving it a comprehensive dining experience.

When eating linguine with clams on the Amalfi Coast, it is vital to be aware of the local customs and etiquette. It is usual to eat with your hands in Italy, but the use of utensils is generally accepted when dining in restaurants. It is also crucial to remember to dress appropriately for the occasion, as many restaurants in the region have a dress code.

Linguine with clams is a wonderful and tasty dish that is a must-try for tourists visiting the Amalfi Coast. The recipe is simple yet tasty and displays the region's cuisine and its love for seafood. Whether you are searching for a light summer supper or a heavy evening, this dish is sure to satisfy you.

Tiramisu

Tiramisu is a renowned Italian dessert that has been loved all over the world. On the Amalfi Coast, it is a mainstay of the local cuisine and is enjoyed by both visitors and locals alike.

Tiramisu is a dessert that developed in the Veneto region of Italy in the mid-20th century. The word "tiramisu" means "lift me up" in Italian, and it is stated that the delicacy was devised as a method to deliver a delicious and invigorating treat to folks who were feeling fatigued or depleted. The dish comprises layers of creamy mascarpone cheese, espresso-soaked ladyfingers, and chocolate powder.

On the Amalfi Coast, tiramisu is cooked with the freshest and finest ingredients, including locally-sourced mascarpone cheese, espresso brewed with beans produced in the neighboring hills, and high-quality cocoa powder. The outcome is a rich and indulgent dessert that is both satisfying and refreshing.

One of the greatest places to have tiramisu on the Amalfi Shore is at one of the many cafes and restaurants that line the streets of the villages along the coast. These places provide a variety of sweet delights, like tiramisu, along with a selection of savory dishes and drinks. When purchasing tiramisu on the Amalfi Coast, it is necessary to keep in mind that it is often made to order, so it may take a few minutes for it to be produced.

Tiramisu is also available in many of the local gelaterias, or ice cream stores, around the region. These shops provide a choice of gelato varieties, including tiramisu that is created with the freshest and finest ingredients. In addition to gelato, many of these stores also sell a selection of other sweet delights, such as cannolis and panna cotta, which are also popular on the Amalfi Coast.

Tiramisu is also a famous dessert on the Amalfi Coast due to its adaptability. It can be eaten as a solitary dessert or coupled with a range of other sweet pleasures, such as fresh fruit, pastries, and even savory foods. This versatility makes it a popular choice for travelers who are searching for a sweet and enjoyable way to end their meal, regardless of what else they have ordered.

Tiramisu is a hallmark of the cuisine on the Amalfi Coast and is a must-try for anybody visiting the region. Whether you are searching for a sweet treat to savor after a meal, or simply a delightful dessert to enjoy on its own, tiramisu is guaranteed to please. Be sure to head to one of the many cafés or gelaterias on the Amalfi Coast and treat yourself to a slice of this delicious and energizing dessert on your visit.

Visitors to the Amalfi Coast can enjoy these and other traditional dishes in local restaurants, and many local markets offer fresh ingredients to cook with at home.

Traveling Essentials

To make the most of your journey to this magnificent place, here are some crucial things you should consider bringing with you.

General Essentials

Comfy Shoes

-   With its mountainous landscape and cobblestone streets, the Amalfi Coast necessitates comfortable footwear. Pack shoes that give decent support, as you will be doing a lot of walking.

Sunscreen and Sun Hat

-   The Mediterranean sun may be fierce, especially during the summer months, so make sure you pack good quality sunscreen with a high SPF and a sun hat to protect your skin.

Light, Breathable Clothing

-   The weather on the Amalfi Coast can be warm and humid, especially during the summer, so make sure to pack lightweight, breathable clothing made from natural fibers, such as cotton or linen.

Swimwear

- The beaches on the Amalfi Coast are a
  significant draw, so don't forget to carry a
  swimsuit and beach towel.

Water Bottle

- Stay hydrated by carrying a reusable water bottle
  with you, as the Mediterranean sun may be
  dehydrating.

Camera

- With its gorgeous shoreline and lovely villages,
  the Amalfi Coast is an excellent destination for
  photography. Bring a camera or smartphone with
  an excellent camera to capture your memories.

Trip Adaptor

- Make sure to bring a travel adaptor with you, as
  the outlets in Italy are different from those in
  many other countries.

Cash & Credit Card

- The Amalfi Coast is predominantly a cash-based
  economy, so make sure to have enough cash
  with you for your expenses. A credit card is also

useful for more expensive purchases and for withdrawing cash from ATMs.

Travel Insurance

- Travel insurance is usually a good idea, especially when traveling overseas. Make careful to purchase coverage that covers medical bills and emergency evacuation, in case of an accident or illness.

Hiking Essentials

Hiking in the Amalfi Coast may be a breathtaking experience, with its stunning views of the Mediterranean Sea and the steep landscape. Here are some key items you should pack to make your trek pleasurable and safe:

Good footwear

- Proper footwear is necessary for a good hike on the Amalfi Coast. Choose shoes that are strong, comfy, and provide appropriate support. Hiking boots or trail runners are appropriate as they give traction and stability on rough and uneven terrain.

Clothing

- Dress in layers as the temperature can vary during the day. Light, breathable clothing is appropriate for warmer weather, and a windproof and waterproof jacket is advised for chilly and wet circumstances.

Hydration

- Bring enough water for your hike and make sure to consume lots of fluids before, during, and after your hike. A hydration pack or a water bottle is convenient to bring with you.

Food

-   Pack energy-rich foods, such as fruit, granola bars, and almonds, to power your hike. It's also a good idea to bring a sandwich or a wrap for a more substantial supper.

Sun protection

-   The Amalfi Coast becomes very hot during the summer months, therefore it's vital to protect yourself from the sun. Bring a hat, sunglasses, and sunscreen with a high SPF to keep your skin protected.

First aid kit

-   A modest first aid kit should include band-aids, antiseptic wipes, pain medicines, and any personal prescriptions you may need.

Map and compass

-   A comprehensive map and a compass can help you navigate the trails and guarantee you stay on track. You can also download a GPS navigation app for your phone for added directions.

Headlamp or flashlight

- It's always a good idea to pack a headlamp or flashlight in case you find yourself trekking in the dark or in low-light circumstances.

Trash bag

- Always pack out everything you pack in and leave no trace on the trails. A tiny trash bag can assist you to dispose of any rubbish you make.

Emergency whistle

- A loud whistle might assist you signal for help in an emergency circumstance.

Money and ID

- It's always a good idea to carry some money and your identity in case of an emergency.

Before beginning your hike, make sure to investigate the trail you plan to take and be prepared for the circumstances you may experience. Make sure you are physically fit and comfortable with the level of difficulty of the trail. It's also crucial to be mindful of your surroundings and to keep on approved paths to limit the effect on the ecosystem and reduce the danger of getting lost.

Hiking on the Amalfi Coast is an unforgettable experience, and appropriate preparation is important to make the most of your adventure. Make sure you pack the needed materials and be prepared for the situations you may experience. Happy hiking.

Swimming Essentials

Swimming on the Amalfi Coast, a length of shoreline in Italy, is an exciting and gratifying experience for holidaymakers. However, there are several fundamentals that you should be aware of before diving in.

Safety

- Alwaysculine beaches of the Amalfi Coast may not have lifeguards on duty, so it's vital to be cautious and swim within your boundaries. Be careful of any warnings or flags that signal harmful currents or conditions, and don't swim too far out to sea. If you're not a strong swimmer, consider employing a flotation device, such as a life jacket or inflatable raft.

Weather

- The weather on the Amalfi Coast can change quickly, so it's vital to check the forecast before heading to the beach. During the summer, temperatures can reach into the upper 80s and 90s, making it excellent for swimming. However, heavy gusts and turbulent waters can make it dangerous to swim, so always check the conditions before entering the ocean.

Sun Protection

- The Amalfi Coast is notorious for its harsh sun, so make sure to bring lots of sunscreens and reapply it periodically. Sunburn may be quite uncomfortable, therefore it's crucial to protect your skin from the sun's damaging rays. You can also bring a hat, sunglasses, and a beach towel to provide additional protection and comfort.

Clothing

- When swimming at the Amalfi Coast, it's necessary to dress appropriately. Wear a swimsuit that fits properly and is composed of sturdy and quick-drying material. If you plan on spending a lot of time in the water, consider wearing a rash guard or swim shirt to protect your skin from the sun and any irritation caused by salt water and sand.

Respect the Environment

- The Amalfi Coast is home to a varied array of marine species, therefore it's crucial to be mindful of the environment when swimming. Avoid touching or disturbing aquatic wildlife, such as fish and coral, and dispose of any waste in appropriate bins. This will help safeguard the delicate environment and guarantee that the Amalfi Coast remains a beautiful and healthy location for future generations to enjoy.

Lifeguards and Emergency Services

- Some beaches on the Amalfi Coast may have lifeguards on duty, but it's always vital to be cautious of your surroundings and swim within your boundaries. In case of an emergency, call 112 or the local emergency services.

Snorkeling and Scuba Diving

- If you're interested in exploring the underwater world of the Amalfi Coast, try taking a snorkeling or scuba diving tour. You may discover plenty of guided tours and rental equipment in the local cities and villages. When scuba diving, it's crucial to have sufficient training and certification and to always dive with a companion.

Swimming on the Amalfi Coast is a fantastic experience for tourists, but it's vital to be prepared and informed of the necessities. From safety to weather, sun protection, and respect for the environment, taking the time to familiarize yourself with these basics can help assure a safe and happy swimming experience on the Amalfi Coast.

Traveling Itinerary

Here's are samples of itineraries to make the most of your trip

5 Day Itinerary plan

Here is a sample itinerary for a 5-day trip to the Amalfi Coast.

Day 1: Arrival in Naples and Transfer to Amalfi

- Upon arrival at Naples International Airport, take a shuttle to Amalfi, which is about 2 hours away by automobile. Check into your hotel and spend the rest of the day exploring the lovely town of Amalfi, noted for its small alleyways, pastel-colored houses, and beachfront piazza. Visit the Amalfi Cathedral, dedicated to Saint Andrew, and the exquisite Paper Museum, which highlights the town's history of paper-making.

Day 2: Explore the Amalfi Coast

- Take a boat tour of the Amalfi Coast to admire its breathtaking landscape and see the adjacent villages of Positano, Ravello, and Conca dei

Marini. Positano is also known for its high-end boutiques, while Ravello is a hilltop town famed for its spectacular vistas, lovely gardens, and old mansions. Conca dei Marini is a little fishing community with a gorgeous harbor and various seafood eateries.

Day 3: Visit Pompeii

-   Spend the day seeing the ancient city of Pompeii, located about an hour away from Amalfi. Explore the city's old streets, public baths, residences, and markets, and see the iconic plaster casts of the victims of the eruption.

Day 4: Hike the Path of the Gods

-   Take a picturesque trip along the "Path of the Gods," a well-known walking track that stretches along the Amalfi Coast. The walk offers spectacular views of the coast and surrounding villages and is a terrific opportunity to explore the area's natural beauty. Stop at the villages of Bomerano and Nocelle along the road and enjoy a picnic lunch.

Day 5: Departure

- Spend your final day in Amalfi visiting the town and shopping for gifts. In the late afternoon, take a shuttle back to Naples International Airport for your departing flight.

This itinerary offers a fair mix of cultural, scenic, and outdoor experiences, and may be changed based on your interests and speed.

Some further ideas for the Itinerary include visiting the seashore village of Vietri sul Mare, known for its ceramics, and the town of Maiori, with its long sandy beach and historical center.

2 weeks Traveling Itinerary

If you are planning a two-week vacation here, there are some must-see sights that you won't want to miss. Here is an itinerary for your trip:

Week 1

- Day 1: Arrival in Naples - Upon arrival, take a train or bus to the town of Sorrento, located on the Amalfi Coast. This will be your base for the first week of your vacation.

- Day 2: Explore Sorrento - Start your day with a great Italian breakfast, then spend the day visiting Sorrento. Visit the historic center, Piazza Tasso, and Marina Grande beach.

- Day 3: Pompeii and Mount Vesuvius - Take a day's journey to Pompeii, and explore it. After visiting Pompeii, you can also trek to the top of Mount Vesuvius to experience amazing views of the surrounding area.

- Day 4: Amalfi and Ravello - Take a ferry or drive to the town of Amalfi, located approximately 20 minutes from Sorrento. After spending the day in Amalfi, take a short drive to the village of Ravello to see the views from the famed Villa Rufolo.

- Day 5: Positano - Take a ferry or drive to Positano. Spend the day touring the town's small streets, checking out the local stores and boutiques, and relaxing on one of the many beaches.

- Day 6-7: Free days - Use these two days to rest and explore Sorrento. You can go on a lovely walk along the coast, attend a cooking class, or simply enjoy a glass of local wine on a terrace overlooking the sea.

Week 2

- Day 8: Transfer to Capri - Take a ferry from Sorrento to the island of Capri, located just a few miles off the Amalfi Coast. Capri is recognized for its breathtaking views, gorgeous beaches, and stylish boutiques.

- Day 9: Explore Capri - Spend the day exploring the island, seeing the famous Blue Grotto and taking a gorgeous boat tour of the coast.

- Day 10: Anacapri - Take a short bus ride to the village of Anacapri, located on the highest point of the island. Spend the day appreciating the sights and browsing the local shops and restaurants.

- Day 11-12: Free days - Use these two days to relax and enjoy Capri at your own leisure. You can go on a lovely hike, take a boat excursion, or simply enjoy the island's magnificent beaches.

- Day 13: Return to Sorrento - Take the ferry back to Sorrento and spend the night in the town.

- Day 14: Departure - On your final day, check out of your accommodation and head to the airport for your trip back home.

This is a sample schedule for a two-week trip to the Amalfi Coast. The region is rich in history, culture, and natural beauty, so there are lots of things to see and do during your stay.

1 Month Itinerary

With its stunning landscapes, lovely villages, and rich history, it is a perfect destination for a one-month trip itinerary. Here is a proposed itinerary that will allow you to explore the most of what the Amalfi Coast has to offer:

- Day 1-3: Arrival and Accommodation in Sorrento

  Upon arrival at Naples airport, take a train or bus to Sorrento, a picturesque coastal town that serves as a fantastic base for visiting the Amalfi Coast. Sorrento is well-connected to the rest of the coast by ferry and bus, making it a great starting place for your explorations.

  Spend the first few days of your journey visiting Sorrento, including a visit to the city's ancient center, Piazza Tasso, and the beautiful views of the Bay of Naples from the town's cliff-top gardens. Take a stroll along the lovely marina and enjoy some of the local food in the various restaurants and cafés.

- Day 4-6: Explore the Island of Capri

  Take a ferry from Sorrento to the adjacent Island of Capri, one of the most popular attractions in the Amalfi Coast. The island is famed for its outstanding natural beauty, including the famous Blue Grotto and the lush greenery of the Anacapri Gardens. Take a boat excursion around the island to see the famed Faraglioni rocks and explore the lovely town of Anacapri.

- Day 7-9: Positano and Amalfi

  Take a ferry or bus from Sorrento to Positano, a lovely cliff-side village noted for its colorful buildings and stunning views of the coast. Spend a couple of days visiting Positano, including a hike to the nearby hillside village of Nocelle for panoramic views of the coast.

  From Positano, take a bus to the neighbouring town of Amalfi, another gorgeous seaside town noted for its history and cultural legacy. Explore the town's historic center, featuring the 11th-century church of St. Andrew and the spectacular paper mill museum.

- Day 10-12: Ravello and the neighboring hills

  Take a bus from Amalfi to Ravello, a hillside town that offers spectacular views of the ocean and the surrounding hills. Spend a couple of days touring the town's historic center, including the famed Villa Rufolo and the church of Santa Maria a Gradillo. Take a hike in the neighboring hills to explore the natural beauty of the region, or relax in one of the town's many cafes and gardens.

- Day 13-15: Explore the Archaeological Site of Paestum

Take a train or bus from Sorrento to the nearby town of Paestum, a UNESCO World Heritage Site that is home to one of the best-preserved ancient Greek colonies in Italy. Spend a couple of days exploring the site, including the Temple of Neptune, the Temple of Hera, and the ancient city walls.

- Day 16-18: The Cilento Coast and the Paestum Beaches

Take a bus from Paestum to the nearby town of Agropoli, a delightful coastal town that is noted for its magnificent beaches and historical attractions. Spend a couple of days touring the area, including a visit to the adjacent Paestum Beaches and the ancient ruins of Velia.

- Day 19-21: Explore Naples

Take a train or bus from Sorrento to Naples, the largest city in the region and one of the most historic and cultural cities in Italy. Spend a few days visiting the city, including a visit to the famous National Archaeological Museum and the historic center, which is home to the Castel dell'Ovo, the Piazza del Plebiscito, and the Royal Palace of Naples. Don't forget to try the city's famous pizza, which is considered to be some of the greatest in the world.

- Day 22-24: The Ruins of Pompeii

Take a train or bus from Naples to Pompeii, a famous historical city that was destroyed by the explosion of Mount Vesuvius in 79 AD. Spend a couple of days touring the enormous ruins, which include the Roman amphitheater, the House of the Faun, and the Temple of Jupiter.

- Day 25-27: The Island of Ischia

Take a ferry or hydrofoil from Naples to the adjacent Island of Ischia, a famous resort for its thermal springs and gorgeous scenery. Spend a couple of days visiting the island, including a visit to the Aragonese Castle, the Chiesa Santa Maria a Mare, and the Castello Aragonese.

- Day 28-30: The Amalfi Coast Beaches

Spend the last few days of your journey lounging on the Amalfi Coast beaches, including the famed Spiaggia Grande in Positano and the Marina del Cantone in Massa Lubrense. Take a boat cruise around the coast to see the gorgeous scenery and enjoy the warm waves of the Mediterranean.

- Day 31: Return Home

    Return to Sorrento and take a train or bus back to Naples airport for your trip back home, with memories of a magnificent one-month adventure on the Amalfi Coast.

Whether you're interested in history, culture, or natural beauty, this itinerary will help you make the most of your stay in the region and enjoy the best that Italy has to offer.

Amalfi Coast On a Budget

While it is often considered a more affluent resort, it is feasible to visit the Amalfi Coast on a budget and have a good experience.

One of the best ways to save money on your trip is to choose your lodging carefully. Instead of staying in a hotel in one of the more touristy towns, consider staying in a more budget-friendly option like a hostel or a bed & breakfast. If you're going with a group, you can also consider renting a holiday apartment.

When it comes to food, you can save money by eating like a native. Try dining at tiny, family-owned restaurants that provide regional delicacies, or take advantage of the many street food sellers selling great and economical options like pizza and gelato. If you want to cook your own meals, you can acquire fresh ingredients from local markets and shops.

While using the bus is frequently the cheapest way to get around, you may also rent a scooter or a bike to explore the coast at your own pace. If you're traveling between towns, consider taking a ferry instead of a more expensive taxi or tour.

Once you're on the Coast, there are plenty of budget-friendly activities to do. Take a trek along the picturesque cliffs, see the many charming villages that dot the coast, and explore the local markets and stores. If you're interested in history and culture, you may explore the many historical and religious monuments in the vicinity, including the majestic Amalfi Cathedral and the ancient Roman ruins of Pompeii.

When it comes to beach time, there are plenty of free public beaches along the coast, or you may select a private beach club or a beach with a bar or restaurant for a nominal price. The town of Amalfi is particularly noted for its gorgeous beaches and crystal-clear waters.

While a trip to the Amalfi Coast may not be the cheapest vacation option, with a little bit of forethought and a willingness to explore and try new things, it is possible to enjoy this amazing location on a budget. Whether you're interested in outdoor adventure, historical and cultural exploration, or just soaking up the sun and the gorgeous surroundings, there is something for everyone on the Amalfi Coast.

Another option to save money while enjoying the Amalfi Coast is to arrange your activities in advance. Many famous sites and tours offer discounts for reserving online, and you may even take advantage of packages that include various activities at a lesser cost.

One budget-friendly activity that should not be missed is visiting the picturesque and quiet Ravello, a village set high on a cliff overlooking the sea. The town is noted for its magnificent gardens, elegant mansions, and attractive restaurants and boutiques. The Ravello Music Festival is definitely a must-visit, offering concerts and performances in a unique and gorgeous environment.

Another budget-friendly option is to take a boat excursion around the coast, which allows you to experience the gorgeous countryside from a fresh perspective and visit secluded coves and beaches that are not accessible by land. The Amalfi Coast is also home to various environmental reserves, including the Parco Naturale Regionale dei Monti Lattari, which offers ample chances for trekking, bird-watching, and wildlife observation.

Finally, shopping is another opportunity to experience the Amalfi Coast on a budget. The region is famed for its handcrafted ceramics, leather goods, and local delicacies like limoncello, which can all be obtained at a fair price. The local markets and shops are terrific places to find unusual souvenirs and gifts to bring back home.

A journey to the Amalfi Coast does not have to be pricey. With a bit of organization, ingenuity, and budget-conscious decision-making, it is possible to have a memorable and delightful holiday in this magnificent location.

Getting Around Amalfi Coast

The easiest method to tour the area is by renting a car, taking public transportation, or hiring a private driver.

Renting a car

- Renting a car provides you the opportunity to explore the coast at your own speed. You can travel down the winding roads that give spectacular views of the coastline and stop at numerous locations along the way. The roads in the area can be small and steep, so it's necessary to have a strong understanding of driving in hilly terrain. It's also crucial to understand that some routes are closed to automobiles during the summer months.

Public Transportation

- The Sita bus is the principal method of public transportation on the Amalfi Coast. It's a reliable and cost-effective way to move about, but may also be time-consuming due to the many stops along the trip. Another option is the Circumvesuviana train, which runs along the coast and is a convenient way to get between the towns of Sorrento, Pompeii, Herculaneum, and Naples.

Private Driver

- Hiring a private driver is a simple method to tour the Amalfi Coast. A driver will pick you up at your hotel and take you to the destinations of your choice. This is a terrific alternative for individuals who want to sit back and enjoy the scenery without having to worry about navigating the roads.

- Ferries and boats are another means to travel along the Amalfi Coast. There are frequent ferry services that travel between the cities of Amalfi, Positano, and Capri. This is a terrific way to enjoy the sights from the shore and avoid the traffic on the roads.

When going by automobile, it's vital to keep in mind that parking can be restricted in attractive cities along the coast. Most towns have dedicated parking places, however, they can fill up quickly during the high tourist season.

The town of Sorrento is a popular location for those who want to explore the adjacent ruins of Pompeii and Herculaneum. Sorrento is a lovely town with a rich history and is famed.

The Amalfi Coast is also home to a number of spectacular beaches, including the Spiaggia Grande in

Positano, the Marina del Cantone in Nerano, and the Praiano beach.

Whether you choose to explore on your own or with a guide, there are various ways to see the area and appreciate its beauty. It's crucial to plan your vacation in advance to ensure that you have enough time to see all of the attractions and enjoy the many activities offered in the area.

Best Time to Visit Amalfi Coast

The best time to visit the Amalfi Coast depends on various things, including the type of activities you plan to undertake, the weather conditions, and the crowds.

Spring (March to May): is a good season to visit the Amalfi Coast for those who want to avoid the summer heat and crowds. The weather is pleasant, with temperatures ranging from 20°C to 25°C, making it suitable for outdoor activities such as hiking, touring, and visiting the many villages along the coast. During this time, the beautiful flowers of the region are in full bloom, adding to the splendor of the place. However, spring can sometimes bring sudden rain showers, so it's a good idea to pack a light raincoat.

Summer (June to August): is the peak tourist season on the Amalfi Coast, and temperatures can reach up to 30°C. This is the greatest season for beach-goers, as the weather is pleasant and the beaches are at their busiest. The summer months are also a terrific time for outside dining and savoring the local seafood. However, the crowds might be overpowering, and it may be difficult to locate a quiet space to rest.

Fall (September to November): is another fantastic time to visit the Amalfi Coast, as the weather is still nice, but the crowds have thinned down. The temperatures during this period are normally in the mid-20s, making it perfect for outdoor activities such as hiking, sightseeing, and boat rides. The fall is also a fantastic time to experience the local food since the area is famed for its delicious fresh produce, notably tomatoes, olives, and grapes.

Winter (December to February): is the off-season on the Amalfi Coast, and temperatures can dip to as low as 10°C. Although the weather is cooler, the Amalfi Coast is still a terrific option for people who wish to escape the crowds and enjoy the tranquil beauty of the country. During this time, the area is perfect for touring, as the streets are calmer and the villages are decked for the Christmas season. However, some tourist attractions and restaurants may be closed during this time, so it's crucial to prepare beforehand.

When planning your trip to the Amalfi Coast, it's vital to keep in mind that some of the communities, like Positano and Amalfi, can be congested and crowded, especially during peak tourist season. To avoid the crowds, consider visiting the smaller communities along the shore, such as Praiano or Conca dei Marini, which provide a more relaxing and authentic experience.

For those interested in outdoor sports, the Amalfi Coast is also an excellent place for hiking and trekking. The coast "Path of the God's", route is best appreciated in the early morning or late afternoon, when the crowds are smaller. The Amalfi Coast is also noted for its superb water sports, including swimming, snorkeling, and scuba diving.

When it comes to dining and nightlife, the Amalfi Coast provides a range of alternatives, from informal coastal restaurants to high-end dining venues. The region is noted for its fresh seafood and traditional Italian cuisine, and there are many restaurants and cafes along the shore where you may experience the local specialties. At night, the villages come alive with pubs and nightclubs, offering a lively environment and a chance to dance the night away.

Finally, it's vital to understand that the Amalfi Coast can be tough to move around, as the roads are tiny and twisting, and public transportation might be restricted. For this reason, it's advisable to rent a car or arrange a private trip to completely explore the area.

The best time to visit the Amalfi Coast depends on what you want to do and your particular tastes. If you want to enjoy the pleasant weather and the beaches, summer is the finest season. If you want to avoid the crowds and appreciate the region's beauty, spring or fall is the best time. If you prefer a quiet and serene trip, winter is a good option. No matter when you visit, the Amalfi Coast is likely to impress you.

Nightlife on Amalfi Coast

One of the most popular towns for nightlife is Amalfi itself, which is home to a variety of bars, clubs, and live music venues that stay open late into the night. For a more upmarket experience, Positano is a popular choice, with sophisticated pubs and restaurants that offer stunning views of the coast. Ravello, on the other hand, is famed for its classical music concerts and classical music performances that take place in the old houses and gardens.

In Amalfi, the main piazza Piazza del Duomo is a center of activity at night, with street performers and live music filling the air. The town is also home to a variety of bars, notably La Conchiglia, that offer spectacular views of the coast and a vibrant environment. Another famous spot is Bar Internazionale, which is noted for its cocktails and live music.

Positano, with its tiny, winding alleys and stunning beaches, is also a favorite location for nightlife. The town is home to a number of pubs, including Music on the Rocks, a fashionable club that sits atop a cliff overlooking the sea and features live music and DJs. Another famous site is Il San Pietro di Positano, a trendy pub that offers a panoramic view of the coast and a refined environment.

In addition to pubs and clubs, the Coast is also home to a number of restaurants that give a vibrant scene at night. Some of the most popular dining venues include La Conchiglia, which serves classic Italian cuisine, and Da Gemma, which is famed for its seafood specialties and breathtaking vistas.

For those searching for a more laid-back nighttime experience, there are also a number of beaches and piers along the coast that give spectacular views of the water and make a fantastic site for viewing the sunset. The beaches of Praiano and Conca dei Marini are popular sites for relaxing and soaking in the breathtaking views of the coast.

Amalfi Coast also provides numerous unique experiences that are not to be missed. One of these is the Limoncello Festival, which takes place each year in the town of Sorrento. The festival is dedicated to the iconic Italian liqueur, Limoncello, and incorporates live music, food, and drink stalls, as well as Limoncello tastings and workshops.

For those who want a more cultural experience, the Amalfi Coast is home to a variety of antique churches and castles that come to life at night with beautiful light displays. The Building of Amalfi, for example, is a gorgeous cathedral that is lit up at night, offering a breathtaking backdrop for a night out on the town. The Castle of Ravello, a medieval fortification that was built in the 10th century, is another favorite place for a night of cultural exploration.

Another favorite nocturnal activity on the Amalfi Coast is boat trips, which give beautiful views of the coastline and provide a unique perspective of the cities and villages that dot the coast. From individual boat tours to group excursions, there is a range of alternatives available, each presenting a different perspective of the shore.

The nightlife on the Amalfi Coast is dynamic, eclectic, and full of unique experiences that are not to be missed. Whether you're seeking for live music, a cultural experience, or simply a magnificent view, the Amalfi Coast has something for everyone. So if you're planning a trip to this gorgeous section of Italy, be sure to carve out some time to explore the coast after dark.

Amalfi Coast Souvenirs

Tourists visiting the area typically prefer to bring back mementos as a reminder of their vacation.

Limoncello

- Limoncello is a must-try for anybody visiting the Amalfi Coast and makes for a fantastic gift for friends and family back home.

Ceramics

- The Amalfi Coast is famed for its ceramics, which are handmade and painted with vibrant colors and beautiful designs. You can discover a range of ceramic products, including vases, plates, and tiles.

Leather items

- Leather goods such as bags, wallets, and sandals are very popular souvenirs. They are manufactured from high-quality leather and are often handcrafted by local artists.

Jewelry

- Jewelry fashioned from coral and other native materials is a frequent memento. These objects are generally one-of-a-kind and make for a great and unusual present.

Food goods

- Food items like olive oil, pasta, and local spices are particularly popular mementos. They are a terrific way to bring the flavors of the Amalfi Coast back home.

Amalfi Coast offers a wide choice of souvenirs for travelers, including liqueurs, ceramics, leather products, jewelry, and food items, all of which embody the essence of the area's culture and history.

Popular Places To Get Souvenirs

Here are some popular venues for travelers to purchase souvenirs:

Positano

- Positano is noted for its boutiques and shops that sell handmade goods, including ceramics, jewelry, and apparel.

Amalfi

- In Amalfi, visitors can find gifts at the famed paper mills, which make high-quality paper made from local materials. Amalfi is also home to various artisan stores that sell handmade ceramics, jewelry, and leather goods.

Ravello

- Ravello is noted for its high-end boutiques and shops that sell expensive goods, including jewelry and textiles.

Sorrento
- Sorrento is noted for its artist workshops that manufacture handmade pottery, inlaid wood, and other crafts. Visitors can also find a range of food goods, including limoncello, olive oil, and spices.

Naples

- While not located on the Amalfi Coast, Naples is a nearby city that offers a multitude of shopping choices, including souvenirs. Visitors can find a range of handicrafts, including ceramics, jewelry, and leather goods, as well as local cuisine items.

These are just a few of the many places where travelers visiting the Amalfi Coast can purchase mementos. Whether you're looking for handmade crafts or gourmet culinary items, you're sure to find something that meets your taste and budget.

Tourist Safety Tips

With its cliff-side settlements, crystal clear waterways, and magnificent surroundings, it is a must-visit for vacationers. However, travelers should take essential steps to guarantee their safety while enjoying this lovely region. Here are some safety recommendations to bear in mind while visiting the Amalfi Coast:

Be wary of pickpockets

-   Pickpocketing is a typical occurrence in tourist-heavy regions such as the Amalfi Coast. To avoid being a victim, store your valuables, such as your wallet and phone, in a secure location and be vigilant of your surroundings.

Wear proper footwear

-   The Amalfi Coast is notorious for its steep and narrow streets, so it is necessary to wear comfortable and durable footwear that gives good traction. Flip-flops, sandals, or high heels are not ideal for these types of streets.

Be cautious when swimming

-   The seas of the Amalfi Coast can be deceptively treacherous, especially for untrained swimmers.

Always swim in designated places and be wary of strong currents and waves.

Take care when driving

- The roads of the Amalfi Coast can be narrow, winding, and steep, so it is vital to be cautious when driving. Always drive at a safe speed and be alert of other vehicles, cyclists, and pedestrians.

Respect local customs

- The Amalfi Coast is a culturally rich location, and it is crucial to respect the customs and traditions of the local people. This includes not snapping images of folks without their permission and wearing modestly when visiting holy locations.

Watch out for scammers

- Scammers are ubiquitous in tourist locations, and the Amalfi Coast is no exception. Be aware of persons who contact you proposing things that appear too good to be true.

Stay hydrated

- The Amalfi Coast can get very hot and humid during the summer months, so it is crucial to stay hydrated. Always bring a water bottle with you and take regular pauses in shaded areas to avoid heat fatigue.

Be prepared for power outages

- Power outages are a typical occurrence on the Amalfi Coast, especially in rural areas. It is a good idea to bring a backup power source, such as a portable charger, to ensure that you have a source of light and communication in case of an interruption.

Stay safe on the water

- Boating is a popular sport in the Amalfi Coast, but it is necessary to take safety precautions. Always wear a life jacket, have a means of communication, and ensure the boat you are using is appropriately outfitted.

Know the emergency services

- It is crucial to know the emergency services available in the area, such as the local police, fire department, and hospital. Make sure you have their contact information easily available in case of an emergency.

The Coast is a lovely area to visit, but it is crucial to take appropriate steps to secure your safety.

By being mindful of pickpocketing, wearing appropriate footwear, being cautious when swimming and driving, respecting local customs, and being hydrated, you can ensure that your trip to the Amalfi Coast is a safe and pleasurable one.

Things To Do In Case of Emergency

Here are some critical procedures to take in case of an emergency at the Amalfi Coast:

Know the local emergency numbers

-   The Italian emergency number is 112, which should be used for all kinds of emergencies, including medical, fire, and police.

Familiarize yourself with the area

-   Before you travel, take some time to familiarize yourself with the area, including the location of hospitals, police stations, and consulates.

Prepare a travel first aid kit

-   Pack a basic first aid kit, including goods such as pain relievers, bandages, antiseptics, and any essential prescription prescriptions.

Learn basic first aid

-   Knowing basic first aid can be handy in case of an emergency. Take a first aid course before your travel.

Have travel insurance

- Make sure you have comprehensive travel insurance before you travel. This will offer you peace of mind in case of any medical crises or other unexpected situations.

Be cautious of the local environment and weather conditions:

- The Amalfi Coast may be hot and humid in the summer months, so it is necessary to stay hydrated and take precautions against sunburn and heat exhaustion. In the winter, there can be significant rains, so be prepared for wet and slippery terrain.

Know the local laws and customs

- Familiarize yourself with the local laws and customs, especially any prohibitions on alcohol and drug usage, and be careful of local views towards foreigners.

Be prepared for natural disasters

- The Amalfi Coast is located in an earthquake zone, so be prepared for probable earthquakes and tsunamis. Keep a watch on the news for any alerts, and know the location of the nearest evacuation shelters.

Stay informed about the local circumstances

- Stay informed about the local situation and any potential dangers, such as protests, strikes, or political instability.

Have a plan for communication

- Make sure you have a plan for communication in case of an emergency. This may entail having an international phone plan or a local SIM card and making sure your friends and family know how to contact you.

In case of a medical emergency, seek aid immediately by phoning 112. If you are in a remote place, it may take some time for aid to arrive, so it is crucial to keep calm and take actions to care for yourself or anyone else who is harmed. If you have travel insurance, follow their recommendations for seeking medical care. If you need to be hospitalized, make sure to bring your passport, travel insurance information, and any essential medical papers with you.

In case of a fire, call 112 immediately and exit the building. If you are in a hotel or other public building, follow the evacuation protocols and stay away from the building until the fire has been extinguished.

In case of theft or loss of personal items, report the event to the local police. Make sure to carry a copy of your passport and travel insurance information with you, and keep a record of the specifics of the theft or loss.

By being prepared and understanding what to do in case of an emergency, you can have a safe and happy trip to the Amalfi Coast. Remember to be informed, have a strategy for communication, and be careful of local laws and customs.

Festival and Events in the Coast

The region is steeped in history, art, and culture and holds various festivals and events throughout the year that exhibit its distinct legacy and beauty.

Amalfi Coast Music Event

- This festival is held yearly in June and is dedicated to classical music. It is one of the most prominent classical music events in Italy and attracts guests from all over the world. The event is hosted in the town of Ravello and comprises music in the lovely surroundings of the Villa Rufolo and Villa Cimbrone.

Saint Andrew's Event

- This festival is held on the 30th of November and is dedicated to Saint Andrew, the patron saint of Amalfi. The festival is celebrated in the town of Amalfi and comprises a procession of boats that carry a statue of Saint Andrew out to sea.

Ravello Festival

- This festival is conducted yearly in July and August and is one of the oldest cultural events in Italy. It comprises concerts, exhibitions, and performances by artists from all around the world. The event is hosted in the town of Ravello which is famed for its breathtaking views of the Amalfi Coast.

Feast of the Assumption

- This feast is commemorated on the 15th of August and is devoted to the Virgin Mary. It is celebrated at the town of Atrani and comprises a procession of boats bringing a statue of the Virgin Mary out to sea.

Feast of the Rosary

- This event is commemorated on the 7th of October and is devoted to the Virgin Mary. It is celebrated in the town of Furore and comprises a procession of boats bringing a statue of the Virgin Mary out to sea.

These are some of the most prominent festivals and events on the Coast. Visitors can discover the rich culture and history of the region and enjoy the breathtaking views of the coastline while participating in these events. Whether you are interested in classical music, fashion, or religious celebrations, the Amalfi Coast has something to offer you.

Printed in Great Britain
by Amazon

19783489R00088